THE PARENT'S TOOLKIT

Simple & Effective Ways to Help Your Child Be Their Best

Naomi Richards

Vermilion
LONDON

1 3 5 7 9 10 8 6 4 2

This edition published 2012 by Vermilion, an imprint of
Ebury Publishing
A Random House Group company

The Random House Group Limited Reg. No. 954009

Addresses for companies within the Random House Group can be found
at www.randomhouse.co.uk

The Random House Group Limited supports The Forest
Stewardship Council (FSC®), the leading international forest
certification organisation. Our books carrying the FSC label are
printed on FSC® certified paper. FSC is the only forest certification
scheme endorsed by the leading environmental organisations,
including Greenpeace. Our paper procurement policy can be found
at www.randomhouse.co.uk/environment

MIX
Paper from
responsible sources
FSC® C016897

Printed and bound by CPI Group (UK) Ltd, Croydon, CR0 4YY

ISBN 9780091940157

To buy books by your favourite authors and register for offers visit
www.randomhouse.co.uk

For my boys – D, E and K

Contents

Introduction

Hi, my name is Naomi Richards and to my knowledge I am the only life coach in the UK that works with children as young as six years old. If you search the internet, you will notice that there are several life coaches who work with teenagers or there are coaches for parents, but when it comes to life coaches for children of primary school age, it seems that I am the only one in the country! The reason for this may be simple. It may be because life coaching children is fairly new in the UK and with anything new it takes time for something to catch on. Life coaching for children is huge in the USA and lots of children have them. There is no stigma attached to having one – the coaching process is seen as a progressive and positive one for children to be able to solve their own problems. It is also popular because it is very different to counselling. There are many differences between counselling and coaching but one of the main ones is that counselling focuses on a person's past whereas coaching is all about looking forward and making changes today for the future.

I think life coaching for children sounds quite ambiguous so I have some examples of how I would describe my job:

- I coach children to find practical solutions to their problems.
- I give children the skills/tools they need for life.
- I help children with their troubles and worries using coaching principles.
- I address the here and now of a child's problems.
- I get children to believe that they can change the situations they find themselves in.
- I work alongside children, encouraging them to be better communicators/thinkers.
- I help children with their difficulties, their fears and their thoughts.

I think these definitions really do explain what my job is all about and I hope some or all of them will resonate with you.

Why do parents want a life coach for their children?

It is always the parents that initiate that their child comes and sees me and most of the children welcome the idea of talking through their thoughts and fears with an impartial stranger. There was a time when children had grandparents or aunts around to talk to, but nowadays families are more fragmented geographically. Some children do not have anyone they can talk to or help with their problems.

Parents approach me for four reasons:

- Their child has a problem and they don't know how to help them with it.
- The parents notice that their child has a problem but the child won't talk to them.
- The parents want their child to change their behaviour.
- The parents feel that their child needs to learn new skills.

Whichever reason it is I can help them. In this book I want to give you the skills to be able to help your child.

It would be great if as parents we had all the answers, but we don't. The parenting journey, I find, is a daily on-going challenge. We are constantly learning new things about our children and about ourselves as parents. We have to use our instincts, sometimes quickly, and hope that they are right, and we have to consider our children's feelings and thoughts as well as making sure the rest of our family are happy and safe and have what they need. Parenting is a full-time job and one that carries so many different emotions – I find that I can be on the end of a cuddle one moment and on the end of an angry outburst the next. Our children's moods are incredibly variable and their moods can have an impact on the way we behave and interact with them.

Rewarding process

Coaching children is a very rewarding process – after all, we are helping the future generation change their negative thoughts, feelings and situations into ones that are far more positive and constructive. Children want to understand themselves better and find that through coaching they can become clear about what they really want from life. Life coaching can strengthen their self-confidence and enable them to cope better with school pressures, home life and relationships.

Children can have problem-solving skills but they do not always know how to use them – they sometimes need guidance. They need someone to sit down with them, talk about the problem and then think of the ways they can solve that problem. That person can be you. You are a person they respect and trust and, as well as their parent, you can also be their coach who guides them through their problems. Children need to be able to problem solve as they are going to have to make decisions on their own regarding their work, relationships, where they live, etc. later on in life. Even when they are at primary school they are going to have to stand on their own two feet, so it is never too early to start working with them as their 'coach' to provide them with these essential 'life tools'. If you don't then you may have a child who comes to you for every decision that they have to make.

Guiding your child through their problems

Children are typically interested in addressing real-time problems and solving them quickly. They would rather do this than embark on solutions that require long-term work. They just don't have the patience. They are concerned about their problem today and they want it to disappear before tomorrow. When a problem does not go away it can make a child feel stuck in a rut and it can affect their moods in other areas of their lives. Problems at school are brought home and home problems are taken into the school environment. It is like there is no escape.

Children want to feel valued, respected and listened to by their parents. When they are, they are more likely to return the respect and be cooperative. They may be willing to listen to you more and value your thoughts and opinions. You can be that listening ear who can guide them through their problems and give them the tools that they need to move forward in life. By doing so, you will be setting them up to be happy, confident and resilient young adults. With the tools I use in this book, I am going to teach you how as a parent you can also be your child's life coach.

I have written this book to help you learn more about what is going on inside your child's mind, and to help you focus on assisting your child in the areas of life that they worry about. It will help you when you don't know what to say to your child when they bring a problem to you and will also guide you through to a solution that is right for them. There is never one answer to a child's problem – there are lots, hence the importance of exploring all the options before a final decision about how to tackle and solve the problem can be made by the child.

This book is a toolkit of useful materials to get your child to start to talk to you about issues that are upsetting them and looking at how you can solve them together. It is about communication and collaboration. No child wants to feel that they are isolated and have no one to talk to. Children want your time, your understanding and your help to tackle difficult situations that they find themselves in, and unhappy feelings that they may have.

This book applies to anyone who is raising a child, whether they are a grandparent, step-parent, blood relative, carer or guardian. This book is for you! Remember though that I only work with children from the age of six years old and so these activities are mainly for primary age children. If you use them with younger children they may not be as effective as they are with older children.

The format of the book touches on the main areas of children's lives where they need help. It is different to other 'parenting' books because it is about what children need from their parents and their lives (I am going to use the term 'parents' throughout the book because the majority of child carers are parents regardless of their actual origin to becoming a parent).

Working as a team

I have tried to write this book in a relaxed down-to-earth way so that you feel like I am in the room with you. When I coach children I see them on their own but then, with the child's permission, I relay our sessions to their parents. I do this so that the parents are aware of what their child is going to be doing between sessions. It means that together we can work as a team and the parents can keep an eye out for the changes the child is supposed to be making. As you read through this book you will get a sense of teamwork. Coaching is a collaborative process and so you and your child will be part of the same team, working together to find solutions to problems, and there is nothing better than being part of a team for some children. I want you to get a real feel for coaching and reap the successes when you use my techniques with your child.

I have divided the book into the most important areas of a child's life, where in my experience most children tend to need some help. Each chapter focuses on one main area and umbrellas other related topics. I have included lots of case studies, which I hope will mirror some of the situations that are going on in your household right now, and give you ideas of how you could talk to your child and address a particular issue. All the examples used are real case studies, but I have changed the names and identifying details of the children to protect their identity.

I have also added lots of questions throughout the book to get you to reflect on a subject. Wherever you see a light bulb you will see a question, so before you enter into the world of being a coach to your child I would like you to grab a notebook. These questions will ask you to think about your children, what they need help with and prompt you into thinking about how you can help them. You can use the notebook to write down the solution your child is going to try out and then monitor its success rate. You can also write down what has not worked. Your notebook can complement everything I am talking about, and by the time you have finished reading this book it should contain some valuable information about what your child is responsive to and the actions your child will be making from now on. Keep the notebook somewhere safe and date your entries so you can remember when you started taking a particular action. You can then refer to it whenever you need to.

You will also notice some highlighted boxes with the words 'the tool to use' throughout the book. These boxes contain the main tools of each chapter and each tool is an incredibly useful and powerful exercise that you can do with your child to get them to change the situation they are in.

Everything in this book I have used with children I have worked with and I want to share these ideas with you. Not all of them are original but most are. The fact is that they are all now written down on paper, ready to use and can be disguised as your own work!

Some of the ideas mentioned may not be suitable for your child, and when you suggest one of them they may turn their nose up. Do not worry as there will be others you can use that they will be more receptive to. While I am talking about trying out ideas, it takes time for a new one to take effect, so if after a couple of days or weeks you don't think what your child is trying out is working, persevere. It may take a little bit longer.

The Toolkit

chapter one

How to help your child communicate better

'We have two ears and one mouth so that we can listen twice as much as we speak' EPICTETUS

Give them your time to talk

If there is one thing you want in a family it is good communication and it is one of the most common subject areas that children bring up in a coaching session. Children often complain to me that they are not being listened to by their parents or not being heard. For example, they may feel that they have to constantly repeat things or they are not being told about forthcoming events such as play dates, dentist appointments, etc. Some children also feel that their parents are not giving them the time they would like to talk to them. We are all guilty of that to some extent. We know we aren't giving them the time they deserve because they shout at us when we are occupied with something else, they repeat questions to us or they get confused about what they are meant to be doing because we have not explained something clearly enough to them.

On a day-to-day instruction level I often think that if you can set aside more time to explain something to your children once, then *you* won't be wasting time later down the line having to explain something again to them. Communication is very important for any family. Through speaking and listening, you'll be able to learn of your children's wants and needs, iron out any spats or arguments quickly and get to grips with how you can communicate effectively within your family. Remember each family is different so whatever works for one may not work for another. I know families that communicate by writing notes because they don't get to see much of each other and I know others who hold family meetings once a week to talk about issues that the parents and children are not happy about.

So how can we give children our time for them to talk, really talk, to us? When I say really talk to us I mean have a conversation with them where they can express how they feel about things and share their day with you. There are mealtimes, snack times, car journeys, bedtimes, etc. that are all great times to chat and can be a forum to share and swap stories and experiences. Children may be more relaxed at these times and find it easier to open up to you.

In the morning before school and before bed can be good times to talk. Both of these times of the day can be when the worry monster within a child can rear its ugly head. The 'talk' time should be when you feel your child is going to be responsive and a willing participant in a conversation, as well as when you have the time to talk. When talking with them take as long as your child needs and don't rush them. It may mean that they go to sleep 10 minutes later than usual, but this is better than them not being able to go to sleep because they have something on their mind. Whatever they say to you is important to them so hear them out and let them speak until they have finished. I am not sure there can be a limit of having 'talk' time with your children. I think that what is important is that your child knows they hold your full attention so try and make sure you are not interrupted by anyone else, or by the phone or the doorbell. When I am talking to my children I don't want to be distracted. I want us both to remain focused and for them to feel that there is nothing more important happening at that moment than our conversation.

How much out of 10 do you rate the current communication in your house?

What is the best time of day for you to talk with your children?

Addressing and acknowledging their feelings

Part of the process of having a chat and catch-up with your children is to check that they are okay with everything that is going on in their lives. I will often ask my children, 'How's school?' 'What happened today?' and I try and pick up from them their feelings and go with what they are saying and not saying. There may be something that you want to talk to them about. For example, they may have behaved inappropriately that day. Think first about the way you want to address the issue and how you are going to talk to your child – what kind of voice could you use, what kind of words and how will you broach their feelings? Ask them open-ended questions about the subject so they don't give you yes and no answers.

HOW TO ASK YOUR CHILD OPEN-ENDED QUESTIONS

The conversation could start any of these ways:

'I have noticed you have been a bit upset recently. How is school at the moment?'

'How is your friendship with … as you haven't mentioned her for ages?'

'You seem to be stressed at the moment about your exams. I have lots of ideas about how we can make you less stressed. Would you like to hear some?'

'How are things at school? How are you getting on with friends? How is the work? Which parts are you finding difficult?'

'How do you feel about … ?'

If your child confuses their feelings and thoughts – which they often do – you can pay particular attention to the changes in emotion that your child shows and then identify the emotion back to them – for example, 'You seem to be thinking about something that is making you sad,' – which should then prompt your child to say something about how they are feeling.

In all cases of problem solving parents need to show empathy and understanding of the issue so that your child feels they are supported emotionally. Getting your child to share their worries and troubles is good for them. It makes them feel like they are carrying a lighter load. Even if they don't want or need your help it is always good for them to know you are there with a listening ear.

Do they want your help with problem solving?

As the conversation opens up it may be that your child starts talking about a problem they have, but they have not asked for your help in resolving it. Ask them if they would like your help or if they just want you to listen. It may be that they want to share their ideas of what they plan to do about the problem and want some reassurance from you that they are going to do the right thing. Some children will tell me they have a problem but don't want to do anything about it. For most children, though, it is likely that they are looking for a solution.

THE TOOL TO USE

Problem solving tool

1 Ask your child what they think they could do about their problem.

2 Get them to think of as many solutions as possible.

3 Write the solutions down.

4 Discuss each solution in detail. What does your child think would be the potential outcomes of each one? What would happen if they did x solution or how would the other person react? This will prepare your child for expected and unexpected outcomes.

5 Ask your child to rate each potential outcome out of 10.

6 By looking at these scores, which one or ones are the likeliest solutions to work for them?

7 Can they see anything that may stop them solving the problem? If so discuss and overcome the obstacle.

8 When could they try it out – that day or that week?

9 Ask them how would they know it had worked.

With a bit of help and encouragement from you they will be more likely to try out their new problem-solving technique. Once they have tried it out, ask them how they got on and if it worked. If it didn't work ask them to choose another idea that may be more suitable. Whichever idea they want to try out, support their decision. Remember it is their problem and they will know what is going to work best for them.

An example of this is John finding the right solution to his problem.

John felt really stressed in the morning because he had so much to do before leaving for school. He had to do outstanding homework, eat breakfast, shower, get his bag ready, etc. and because he had so little time he felt stressed about getting it all done. He wanted to have more relaxing mornings. We came up with the following possible solutions:

A Get his school bag ready the night before.

B Have a shower the night before.

C Get up when his alarm goes off.

D Set his clock so that it was half an hour too fast.

E Finish his homework the night before.

We looked at the feasibility of each solution and graded them all out of 10. The idea with the highest mark was going to be the one to try out.

SOLUTION	FEASIBILITY	GRADE
A Get his school bag ready the night before	Good idea	9/10
B Have a shower the night before	Prefer to shower am	6/10
C Get up when his alarm goes off	Yes, stop being so lazy	8/10
D Set his clock so it was half an hour too fast	Won't make a difference	3/10
E Finish his homework the night before	Good idea	9/10

John decided that he would do his homework the night before and get his school bag ready, which meant he had an extra 20 minutes in the morning to do everything else.

You could also get your child to think about the consequences of each solution, should they put it into practice, and write them down on a piece of paper (i.e. what would happen if they tried out each solution?). What would the negative consequences be and what would the positive consequences be? Your child can then balance up in their minds what the best option would be. If we take the example above the piece of paper would look like this:

	NEGATIVES	POSITIVES
A Get school bag ready night before	Less time for TV	More time in morning
B Have shower night before	Like to shower am	More time in morning
C Get up when alarm goes off	Needs his sleep	Not so rushed
D Set clock so it is half an hour fast	Confusing	Ready for school
E Finish homework night before	Less time for TV	More time in morning

Can you think of a problem your child has and think of a way to help them solve it?

Ask them the right questions

As children often find it difficult to identify and vocalise their thoughts, they are more likely to tell you how they feel while doing an activity. I like to talk to my children when they are slightly distracted, such as when we are preparing or cooking dinner or making biscuits. I even like to chat with my children when we are driving somewhere together. They are more relaxed and willing to talk about their thoughts and feelings because there is no direct eye contact and there is no intense focus on them.

Earlier I made some suggestions about how to get children to start talking and mentioned open questions. An open question does not give your child the option of answering with a 'yes' or 'no' answer. An open question means that your child has to give a more detailed answer. For example, 'What did you do at school today?' or, 'Tell me about bowling' warrants at least one sentence.

Open questions all start with a why, what, where, how or when, but you do need to be careful. Ask your child just a few questions rather than bombard them. Children hate being asked question after question. It can make them feel like they are being interrogated.

If your child doesn't want to talk to you, you could guess what they would say in reply to a question you have asked and see if they agree with the response.

Alternatively, you could leave the conversation open and let them come back to you later on with an answer. If you are not in the habit of talking to your child on a regular basis don't expect them to open up to you straightaway. It may take time for them to adjust to you taking an interest in what they are doing and asking them questions. However, don't give up. Keep maximising opportunities for your child to talk and maybe they will take advantage of one of them!

When your child's behaviour changes it means they are feeling something (positive or negative) and that could mean it is time to talk!

Are you giving your child your full attention?

Children often feel that they aren't being listened to because of what we are doing or not doing while they are talking. We can be on the phone, having a conversation with another one of our children, doing domestic chores, etc. – the list is endless because most parents lead incredibly busy lives and try to do more than one thing at a time.

How often does your child tell you that you aren't listening to them? I know in my house it is at least once a week. Have you ever thought why they say that?

- Is it because you are not looking at them while they are speaking?
- Is it because you aren't validating their feelings or thoughts?
- Are you nodding your head? It is good to nod as it shows you are listening.
- Are you distracted by something or someone else?
- Are you saying all those acknowledgement words such as 'oh yes' and 'really'?
- Do you probe them with questions?
- Is it because you jump in with your thoughts or questions about what they are saying before your child has finished talking?

By listening to your child and what they have to say you are showing them respect, and this is a skill that you want them to inherit. Let them speak, don't jump in and make sure you are looking at them when they are talking. Most children will say that if you are not looking at them then you cannot be listening. Ask them questions at the end – they prefer you to do this rather than keep interrupting them. If you ask questions they can lose their train of thought and may get annoyed that you have thrown them off track. Finally, use some great non-verbal and verbal communication such as nodding and saying, 'Yes'.

> I now would like you to have a think. What do you currently do when your child is talking to you and what could you do differently?

Is there an alternative to nagging?

There are many children who feel that all their parents do is nag them because their parents ask them repeatedly to do something. They have to ask constantly because they know their child is not doing what they have requested them to do.

We know children hate to be nagged but sometimes the 'nagging' words just slip out of our mouths. In turn our children don't give us the response we want and give us 'attitude' and possibly aggression back. For instance, some children will stop listening or dig their heels in and shout back.

So, what can we do as parents to stop our children hearing us nag? Well, there are other ways to ask your children to do something – ways that children are more receptive to and will cooperate with. Children usually prefer it when you ask them to do something that you also explain why you are asking them to do it. By giving our children a reason for our request they will be more inclined to carry out the action. It also helps if you give them a time for when they have to complete the task. They then know what they have to do and when they have to do it by. For example, we can ask our children to get their books ready for school, before they go to bed. They may not do it, but if you explain that they will not have to get up early in the morning to get their books ready for school, and that means no nagging by you, it may be the motivation they need to get it done. Children generally want to see or hear about the benefit of what it is you are asking them to do.

Another example of this sort of interaction can be seen in the behaviour of a parent of a child I was working with. The mum told her daughter to wait in the car so that she could pay me after the child's coaching session. The child did not want to so the mum kept on telling her to get into the car. After several times, she bribed her daughter to get in. Slightly embarrassed about the situation, she asked me, 'What else could I have done?' I replied, 'You could have told her that we were going to be two minutes and asked her if she wanted to wait patiently with us or wait for you in the car.' The mum liked the idea of giving her child an option and she tried it out after the next session and it worked. Her daughter chose to wait in the car.

Using the right words

If we use the right words with children we can get good responses. When thinking about the words that children prefer to hear I came across one that can actually benefit both parents and children. It is a word that children respond well to as it is neither a positive or negative word. The word is 'and'. If you change the word 'but' with 'and' you will always be able to praise your child without criticism. For example, if you said, 'We like what you've done but you have missed out . . . ' it doesn't sound as good as saying, 'We like what you have done and if you add in this bit it would be even better . . . .'

I really like the sound of 'and' and so do my children. I like it so much that I have kicked 'but' out of my vocabulary and replaced it with 'and'. And it works. I get more cooperation from my children and they don't feel saddened by the 'but'. I feel that 'but' can be such a negative word and it sounds like a criticism is coming next.

☞ Replace **'but'** with **'and'**.

There is another word that I also find very effective and one that I would also love to share with you and that is the word 'when'. You can replace 'if' with 'when' and get a much better response from your children. For example, 'When you have finished your dinner you can have a yogurt' sounds less conditional than saying, 'If you . . .'. 'If' sounds like a threat doesn't it? The word 'when' gets you exactly what you want from your child. In this case it is getting them to eat all of their main course before they can have dessert.

☞ Replace 'if' with 'when'.

Both are great words to use in communication as they are positive.

> Which words do you use so your children will be more cooperative?

If you don't already use 'and' and 'when' try using them and write down how responsive your children are towards them.

Helping children who have a tendency to talk too much

Some children just love to talk. Not because they love the sound of their own voice but they have so much to say. For example, I often find when I am with my eldest son and his friends that one of them talks non-stop about what they are doing and does not invite the other one into the 'conversation'. The conversation is all one-sided and even if their friend did want to say anything they would not get a word in edgeways. This normally happens with my son and his best girlfriend. They are so excited to see each other that they do not allow the other one to speak. I have had to teach my son about taking turns in conversations – so that a one-sided chat becomes an interesting conversation. I sometimes have to steer the conversations for my son and his friends and say, 'Maybe x would like to say something' or 'What do you (x) think?'

There is a great game that you can play to get children to curb one-way conversations or when children give too much information in response to a question. Ask your child a question and only give them a certain amount of time to answer it (about 10–20 seconds). Use a stopwatch or an egg timer so that they know you are not cheating. Get them to focus on how much information they are providing so they give you the answer you are looking for and no more. You can then take it to the next level, which is to get them involved in a two-way conversation. Ask each other questions, alternately focusing on the questions and the answers provided.

However, it is not just children who talk too much. As parents, we can also be guilty of talking too much when our children ask us questions. So how do we keep our answers short and relevant to them? We can do this by:

- Keeping the answers age appropriate. We know what our children understand and what they don't so use language they are familiar with.

- Giving them just enough information to satisfy their curiosity. If they want more information they will ask another question.

- Keeping the answer short. Long answers may not hold your child's attention.

What changes do you need to make when answering your child's questions?

Not saying enough

If your child feels hounded by you constantly asking them lots of questions why don't you introduce a game to them where they have to talk for a minute about their day, or they have to answer four questions about something they have done. So instead of asking, 'What did you do

today?' and being met with a blank look or a 'No
your child has to say what they did, who they did it w
when they did it and how, why or when? They get to
choose the questions they answer but they have to answer
four. If they cannot remember the questions you can write
these up on a chalk board or a piece of paper and put it on
the fridge or notice board. After a few days they will get the
hang of the game and become more used to telling you
about their day. Perhaps there could be a small forfeit for
them if they don't talk for a minute or answer the four
questions. A good forfeit could be that they have to lay the
table or do a chore for you.

Okay, so now we are listening – but are our children?

Just as we are guilty of not listening, so are our children.
They may not hear us because they don't want to or
because they are absorbed in something else. We have
already talked about why they may not want to listen to us
– it is in the nagging part of this chapter (see page 25). As
for being absorbed in something else we should be able to
gauge this either by going into the room where they are or
by listening to what they are doing. If you want the attention of your child and you know they are doing something
else, go into the room where they are and talk to them
directly. Don't shout between rooms. You would not do it

to your boss at work so why do it to your children? 'Your child will only shout back, 'What did you say?' and then you will have to repeat the instruction.

THE TOOL TO USE
Getting your child to listen

1 If you are in the same room as your child and they are busy get them to look at you by saying, 'Please can you look at me as I would like to talk to you?'

2 If they are distracted by the TV or computer ask them, 'Please can you put it on pause as I would like to talk to you. When I have finished talking you can go back to what you were doing'.

3 Give them the information they need and then ask them to repeat back to you what you have just said. If they can repeat it back to you then you know they have listened. If not, try again.

You could even take the repeating back a step further and make it into a game with you talking about a subject for a few minutes then ask your child to give you five pieces of information that you talked about. Another game I find useful is word association, where you say a word and your child has to say a related word. For example, potato –

carrot – rabbit. It is a good game for memory and listening skills as it will help them focus, concentrate and listen! Try both games out and see how you get on.

To get my children to listen I will sometimes say to them, 'Have you got your listening ears on because I need to talk to you.' This will always make them laugh but it encourages them to listen. Another way is to tell your child that if they do not listen then they may miss some useful information that could be of benefit to them. For example, you may be offering to take them out on an adventure or asking if they want ice cream. If they don't listen they may miss out on an opportunity. Do they want to miss something as important as this?

Communication can be fun

'The secret to humour is surprise' ARISTOTLE

If there is one thing children love it is humour – Mum or Dad joking around, making them laugh. Humour is an amazing way to bond and communicate with your child. It can be used to diffuse or make a situation less serious. I use it to get my children out of a bad mood, use it to get them to eat and use it when they or I make mistakes. For example, if I see a tantrum brewing I may fall on the floor and pretend I am having a tantrum or if I see my son getting angry I can diffuse it quite easily by pulling a face or making a joke. If you have the choice of getting angry and shouting at your child humour is a much better option as it takes the heat out of a situation. Only you know if your child will respond well to humour. If they don't, don't use it!

Non-verbal communication is just as important

> 'According to research, 93% of effective communication is non-verbal. 55% is expressed by body language and 38% by tone, which leaves only 7% for the spoken word'
>
> PROFESSOR ALBERT MEHRABIAN

Wow, that means there is a lot of non-verbal communication going on and I, for one, am all for it. I feel that cuddles, kisses, a cheeky smile, smirk or an encouraging look are just as important as words as they tell our children that they are wonderful, we are proud of them and they make them feel good, loved and secure. I would even go so far as saying that they are part of a child's basic needs after shelter, food and clothes. All these things make children feel able, give them the confidence to try new things and can raise a child's self-esteem. They are free to give but worth their weight in gold to the recipient. Most children love affection but if a kiss and a cuddle are not for them then write them a note to tell them how much you love them and why.

In what format are your children getting non-verbal communication from you?

Checklist

- Find the right time to talk to your children.
- Acknowledge their feelings.
- Ask them the right questions.
- Are you paying attention?
- There is an alternative to nagging.
- Choosing the right words gets a better response.
- Always give an explanation as to why your child has to do something.
- Help your child find the balance of verbal communication.
- Use non-verbal communication.

chapter two

How to encourage self-confidence in your child

'Without self-confidence we are as babes in the cradle'

VIRGINIA WOOLF

What is self-confidence?

Self-confidence is believing in yourself and your abilities. People who are self-confident are more empowered to overcome obstacles that appear in their way. They find it easier to break down barriers and are often more assertive individuals.

On a scale of 1 to 10 with 10 being the most confident and 1 being the least, how confident would you say your child is?

In what area do you think your child could do with a dose of self-confidence?

Who is to blame for your child's lack of self-confidence?

I don't think it is fair to blame one person for your child's lack of confidence. Someone may have said something cruel to them or criticised something they have done. It could have made a dent in their ego and made them feel like they never want to say or attempt to do something again. The damage may make it difficult for them to restore their self-confidence. This someone may be a friend or family member or it may even be you without you knowing it. For example, your son may have had to give a show-and-tell at school and the other children may have laughed at his attempt to talk, or your daughter's friends may have said that she was rubbish at sports. You may have even made a comment like, 'You tried that last time and you weren't very good at it.'

Negative comments

In the scenarios I have mentioned it is how your child receives the comment that is important. If they take the comment to heart it will make them think, 'I don't want to talk in front of the class again' or 'I am not going to do sports again because I am rubbish at it' or 'You are right, I should not try that again.' It may be that one comment makes them feel like this or a combination of comments. In my experience children usually remember the negative things said to them and it can make them feel useless. It takes a resilient child to receive a negative comment, understand, evaluate it and decide if it is useful to them. If it isn't they can disregard it. For example, someone may say to your child that they are a bad sharer and they don't want to play with them any more. This is useful information for your child as it is telling them that they need to share better.

As parents we have a role in nurturing our children to be confident. We can help them on their way by showing them what they are good at and help them to believe in themselves. By using positive phrases and encouraging them in what they can do you will be helping your children to experiment and explore their abilities. This in turn will encourage self-confidence. There are lots of examples and activities in Chapter 6 that you can do with your child to promote self-esteem, which will help with your child's confidence.

The activities will be useful as once a child's confidence is dented they will need help to restore it, because it is not always something that they can do on their own. One of the first things we can do is try and encourage self-confidence from within.

Encouraging self-confidence from within

Children want to be confident to be able to deal with any situation they find themselves in, to be able to 'take care' of themselves in difficult situations and to have the ability to present themselves well. To some children confidence comes naturally; their parents are confident, so they are too. They have seen how their parents deal with certain situations and have learnt from them how they should also react. All children have to learn how to be confident and most of this will be learnt from their parents.

It is important that children develop a positive self-image of their own. A positive image means that they are self-confident, that they know their own limits and trust their own abilities. Children who have a positive self-image have more fun and can handle themselves in tough situations.

Accepting them for who they are

The most important thing we can do is to accept them for the person they are.

THE TOOL TO USE

Acceptance tool

1 Whenever your child does something right or well you should give them great compliments and celebrate their achievement so that they feel encouraged to continue with the job in hand – for example, 'Well done (x) for doing (y)'.

2 When your child does something that is not quite right and they want your help to do better next time then you can advise them as to how they can: 'You did really well last time so let's try and do x to make it even better'.

3 Don't tell them that they did something wrong: 'You did that wrong' and criticise them. You can say to them, 'You know it sometimes takes time to get things right and that every mistake that you make is a learning experience.'

4 Share with your child all the mistakes you have made; I am sure there are plenty! They will see that it really is okay to make errors and that each time you made a mistake or got something wrong that you learnt from the experience.

Our job as parents is not easy when it comes to confidence building but if we can help our children face and deal with a situation that they are not confident about, it could make all the difference to their general confidence. When my oldest son says to me that he is not confident about something, I ask him, 'What is the worst thing that can happen?' We come up with some crazy ideas, and some silly ones too, and he feels so much better. Other confidence-boosting ideas that you may find really useful are outlined in the next section.

Give positive reflections

Children are very responsive to positivity and like to feel valued. Do you give your child the idea that they are fun to be with or that their opinion matters to you? Do you recognise their achievements and talent? If you do, tell them as they will be happy that you noticed. These types of comments are called positive reflections because you are reflecting back on something they have done in the past. A positive reflection can be something such as, 'You did such a great job with your homework' or 'You really helped me out today. You are so helpful.'

Compliments

Compliments can also help with a child's confidence. All children love compliments. They beam from ear to ear to show how proud they are of themselves as a compliment will make them feel good, special and confident about the little and the big things that they are doing well at.

What was the last thing you complimented your child on? How did they respond?

Let children be independent and try new things

There are children who love to try something new and there are those who would rather stick with familiarity. I am going to focus on those children who like a challenge, who want to be independent and try new things.

Your child may want to go on the scariest ride at the theme park or learn karate. Whatever they ask you to try out or experience let them within reason. If you have children like mine, they won't give up asking until you give in! Whether your child is successful or not at their new activity or experience they will have learnt confidence – they have come out of their comfort zone and tried something new and you have shown that you believed they could do it! This can lead to your child attempting more newer experiences and developing more confidence.

How willing are you to let your child try new things?

Confidence is not just about overcoming new experiences. Confidence can come from the way we hold ourselves. I know from my sessions that children will say to me, 'How can I look more confident?' I will then work with them on how they can stand, talk and look confident when in fact inside they are a quivering wreck. How we stand and our posture can really help when we speak. Standing upright can also help project our voice.

Standing tall

When a child comes to me because they find it difficult to talk to other people we discuss body language. Body language does not come easily to some children. They don't want to maintain eye contact because they feel uncomfortable looking into the eyes of someone they may or may not know. They are much happier talking towards the floor or looking out of the window. I think that some children find eye contact quite threatening. Consequently they are looking elsewhere and their body is not facing the person they are speaking to.

Standing tall is essential for looking confident and if your child looks confident they will feel it too. Teach your child to stand with their shoulders back and their head looking straight ahead as if they were being measured against a wall. Bending over and looking at the ground does not breed confidence from the person speaking or from the people listening. If your child is shy or does not have conviction in what they are saying why not practise this at home with them. You can even use humour (my favourite way to get children to do what you want them to do) when they forget to stand tall like, 'Where's my tree?' or 'How does a soldier stand?' It sounds much better than saying, 'Stand up straight.'

Your child may also not be very good at eye contact and as they engage with people all day every day it is quite important. It takes confidence to look into someone else's eyes. Eye contact is one of the most important non-verbal ways for communicating and connecting with other people. Being an extrovert, I love to look into people's eyes. I like to connect with them, as eyes are not only the window to the soul they also answer questions while you are connecting, such as, 'Is this person paying attention to what I'm saying?' or 'Does this person like me?' Having good eye contact with someone shows you are confident about who you are.

I find that not everyone is as comfortable as me with eye contact. It can make some children uncomfortable and feel as if you are staring them out.

I worked with Simon, a lovely 10-year-old, who found eye contact difficult. He was much happier looking down at his feet while talking. We worked together and over the course of a few weeks I got him to look at me while talking. So how did we start and can you get your child to engage with you in this way too?

We started off the session discussing the importance of using eye contact. Why did he think it was necessary to look at someone? What did it tell the other person who was listening? How does he want to feel when someone is talking to him? As we discussed his thoughts and opinions I got Simon to start glancing up while he was talking. He did this by reminding himself that after he had said a few words he needed to look up. It took a lot of conscious action on his part. When I was talking I got him to look at me after every couple of sentences I said and after a couple of sessions he got the hang of it. If he didn't look up enough I would cough to remind him.

His fear of looking someone in the eye tallied with the fact that he did not feel confident in what he was saying. So I worked with him on his eye contact and his conversation at the same time. I asked him why he thought he did not have anything of value to say. Simon said that no one really listened to him and he did not feel that he has a lot to contribute to a conversation. My reaction was, 'You don't know until you try.' Over the course of a few weeks we worked together on building up his confidence. As the weeks went on Simon spoke more, shared his opinions and thoughts and I got him walking around the room looking at me from time to time using his standing tall pose. Result!

As you know my work never stops in the session. I continued to work with his parents so they could make sure that he was mirroring everything we were doing in our sessions outside of them. We would both use key words or give him hints like, 'Who are you talking to?' to remind him to look *at the person who was speaking or to the person he was talking to. Or we would just say, 'Body' to get him to think about what his body and face were doing while talking.*

And smile, smile, smile

Don't they say that when you smile then the rest of the world smiles with you? I believe that smiling makes you look and feel more confident. In the same way you can help your child with their eye contact, so too smiling can be practised. If your child does not like smiling or does not smile a lot, ask them, 'Why don't you like smiling?' and 'How do you feel when someone smiles at you?' I bet it makes them feel great when someone shares a smile with them. So encourage them to do it more!

Smiling tells us that the person we are with likes us. It can also create a great first impression. If your child smiles while they are talking it shows the people they are talking to that they are interested in what they are saying and enjoying the conversation. This is useful for a child to understand when they are perhaps giving a talk in front of their class or just having a chat with friends.

At the beginning of this chapter I asked you to think of where your child feels they lack confidence. Some of the situations you were thinking about may be ones that they find most challenging and back away from. Do you know why your son or daughter backs away? Ask them. It may be because they don't know what to say or it may be that they worry that they will do something and they will be laughed at.

> *For example, Adam would rather not answer a question in class than answer it and possibly get it right. I asked Adam what he was afraid of and he said that he did not want to get the answer wrong. 'How would he feel if he did get it wrong and what would that mean for him?' He would feel sad and a bit embarrassed. 'Now what would happen if he did answer the question right?' He would feel great. 'How would that make him feel and what would be the reaction of the class and teacher now?' The teacher and his classmates would be pleased for him. 'What will he do next time?' Answer the question.*
>
> *For Adam it was all about self-confidence and saying, 'I will have a go. There is a chance the answer will be right'. All it needed was for him to think rationally about the possibilities of getting the answer right and challenging his negative beliefs and thoughts. After a few weeks of trying this out and answering several of the questions right, he realised that actually no one cared or said anything when he got them wrong.*

This is just one example but there are lots of challenging situations your child may not be confident in. I have addressed some of those situations with ideas and possible solutions to build confidence.

Overcoming challenging situations

Walking into a room full of strangers

If your child finds it difficult walking into a room where they don't know many people get them to quickly look around the room and find someone who they vaguely know or someone they like the look of. Talk to them about what they would say to the people they do know and how would they strike up conversation with those that they don't. It could be that they give the person they don't know a compliment, ask their name or ask them what they like doing. You could take it in turns and practise these type of start-up conversations together at home.

START-UP QUESTIONS

'I like your shoes. Where did you get them from?'

'Hi, my name is x, what is yours?'

'Where do you live?'

'What kind of things do you like doing?'

Speaking to an audience or performing in front of other people

It can be very nerve-wracking standing up in front of people you know or don't know and performing. Even as adults we find this difficult. The way that you can help your child overcome this is by getting them to practise by themselves in front of a mirror and then give the talk or performance to you and then to the whole family. It will make them feel more comfortable talking in front of other people. Ask them, 'What would make giving the talk or performance easier?' Would they find it easier to talk or perform and focus on the wall at the back of the room, on an object or perhaps they would prefer to look at one particular person?

I worked with an eight-year-old boy called Joshua who did not feel confident about reading in front of his class. He was worried he would make a mistake or that everyone would laugh at him. What could he do to make himself feel more confident? Could he:

- *Practise in front of Mum – 9/10.*
- *Practise in front of Dad – 3/10.*
- *Read out loud in his bedroom –7/10.*
- *Look at someone he trusts in his class and mainly direct his reading at them – 8/10.*
- *Say to himself on the day that it did not matter if he got a word wrong, everyone makes mistakes – 5/10.*

We discussed each option and graded each idea out of 10. Joshua decided he would practise in front of Mum as she had more patience and would not mind him going over the piece he had to read again and again. Joshua would ask Mum after our coaching session when she had time to do this and if they could do it regularly as part of their time together. On the day he would focus on his friend Ali as he knew Ali would not laugh at him. I saw him again and he said he had managed to do the reading and even enjoyed doing it!

I think one really important issue to mention at this point is when your child shows concern about what they are going to say and thinks everyone will notice if they say something wrong. Reassure them that they are the only one who knows what they are 'supposed' to say and, unless they tell them, no one will know about a mistake they made or a fact they missed out.

> How easy would you say your child finds talking or performing in front of others and which approach do you think would work for them?

Confident in teamwork

Teams bring together children and skills that complement each other. It is good to be part of a team, but some children do not feel confident being part of one because they worry that they are going to let the side down. Building confidence in this situation is about challenging those thoughts your child has. Why do they think they are not good enough? Why would their teacher or friends have chosen them to be a part of it if they were not great at...? Why were they not the first child to be picked to be a partner for a project? Why were they put in a random group by their teacher? Reassure your child that they are good enough and make them realise that they can only do their best. If they don't get the result that they want, they must understand they were working as a team and therefore they are not solely to blame. In some cases where teams were made by a teacher, the teacher will have done so for convenience sake and there was probably no strategy behind the split.

Confident in speaking their mind or in conflict

We don't always agree with what everyone else says. If your child does not agree with someone else's opinion then they can do one of two things. They can keep quiet and not add their opinion or they can speak out and tell the other person what they think, even if that means disagreeing with them. For some children the most obvious choice is for them to agree as they don't want to upset the person by disagreeing. However, by not saying anything at all they are essentially agreeing and possibly compromising themselves. If your child would like to speak up and voice their opinion then ask them why they aren't doing so right now? What is stopping them? Are they worried that no one else will agree with what they have said? What is the worst that can happen?

We need to help children to see that opinions are just that – they are thoughts of other people and that different experiences give us different perspectives on life. Having a discussion and adding your thoughts can be interesting. You are sharing views and quite possibly learning something new about other people.

Being assertive

You can help your child be more assertive by practising these and other types of situations that they find it hard to speak up within. For example, what can they do if their friends are playing football and they don't want to be in goal but they are placed there? What could they say to their friends so they were a midfielder and not in goal? Perhaps they could say, 'I love playing football but I do not like being goalie because ... who will swap with me?'

Or perhaps someone says something to them that they do not like. They could say, 'I really don't like the way you call me ... I am ....' Can they visualise themselves saying or doing this? How would it make them feel? For the examples I have mentioned where children want to feel more confident visualisation is very useful.

Being confident can also be about showing others how you feel and not being afraid to do so. It is not a weakness to show other people how you feel. It takes guts. It also takes guts and confidence to say 'no' to peers. Children can feel very uncomfortable saying 'no' because they want others to like them. They will unhappily give up a go on the Playstation, miss out on food or see a film they don't want to see. By saying 'yes' and not thinking about their own needs your child is not getting what they want and that can make them very frustrated and anxious.

Talk to your child about saying 'no'. They must not be afraid of using that word. They will not be letting others down and the 'no' does not have to hurt anyone. They can say 'no' like this: 'I am sorry I cannot play with you right now. Why don't you go and see if said friend is around as I know they are playing a good game.' Offering a solution is a good alternative.

Having the confidence to be assertive tells your child that they care about themselves, their needs and their happiness. It is okay for them to help other children but if they feel that they are agreeing to doing lots of things for someone else we need to help them to speak up.

Using imagery can create confidence

I love role-playing and imagery. Role-playing can lift a child out of an existing situation into another by acting it out. Role-playing can be fun and can bring out a child's creative side. Imagery is also quite powerful as a child imagines changing a situation for the better and feels the welcome change in their mind. They get a feeling of 'this is what it could be like if I made a change and took responsibility for my actions'.

Role-play and imagery are great ways to practise what your child is going to do and say in a certain situation.

THE TOOL TO USE

Confidence tool

1 Ask your child to stand up straight with their shoulders back and looking at you.

2 Get them to think of something they find difficult to say to a friend, group, etc.

3 Give them a couple of minutes to work out what and how they are going to say it.

4 Get them to imagine they are a superhero who is powerful and has to relay a message to you consisely, confidently and clearly.

5 Ask them to look you in the eye.

6 Tell them to take a deep breath and, feeling how invincible they are, get them to relay their thoughts, feelings and needs to you.

7 How did they feel?

By doing several role-plays your child will be able to practise what they would say and do and be more confident acting it out for real at a later date.

Claire, aged eight, found it really hard to stand up to her big sister who used to walk into the TV room and change channels when Claire was watching a programme. Claire would just let her as she did not see the point of making a fuss. She thought her sister would squash her or say cruel things to her and she did not want that to happen, so she let her change channels despite being angry and upset. I took on the role of Claire and she role-played as her sister as we did some imagery work. I got Claire to imagine how her sister felt having the power to change channels and being allowed. I then got Claire to imagine saying to her sister, 'Actually, I am watching TV', and asking her to wait until she was done. How did she think her sister would react? What would she do if she simply said, 'Okay' or if she put up a fight? What, then? She said it would feel good that she had spoken up although she would have tweaked what she would really say. We talked about what she thought her sister would respond best to and she put it into practise when the situation next occurred.

When I saw Claire at the next session she said that the TV situation had got much better. When her sister went to change channels Claire explained to her that she was in the middle of watching something and that when her programme had finished her sister could have the remote. Claire also suggested that her sister went and watched another one of the TVs in the house. Her sister was shocked

*that she had spoken up and at one point in the week sat
down and watched a programme with her.*

When children imagine what they can have instead of
settling for second best it makes them feel empowered
enough to do something about it.

My final point that I want to make in this chapter is this:
children learn from us. If we are confident in our actions
our children will see and mirror our confidence towards
other people and in 'tricky' situations.

*What are you going to do now to help
your child have more confidence?*

Checklist

- Lack of self-confidence comes from anywhere.
- Accept your children for who they are.
- Give positive reflections.
- Let your children try new things.
- Give them the confidence to speak up.
- Use imagery and visualisation to increase confidence.

chapter three

How to motivate your child to cooperate

'Teamwork divides the task and multiplies the success'

AUTHOR UNKNOWN

Many children I know think that we do not cooperate enough with them. This is mainly because we don't do something straightaway when they ask us to ('What did your last slave die of?' comes to mind). Most children like us to listen to and act on their every need or expect answers from us the moment they have finished asking a question. We do try and cooperate with them as much as we can but sometimes their request is unreasonable or realistic. As a parent you know what is reasonable and what is not, so it is important that you are not pushed around by your children by cooperating with their every demand.

However, what they don't realise is that when we ask them to cooperate with us we are asking because it benefits them and us (e.g. laying the table). Most of the time they won't want to because it is going to take their attention away from something else but if they see that by cooperating dinner will be out on the table much quicker then they will do it. This chapter is not about them cooperating with us, though; it is about us cooperating with them. The way we can do this is to allow them to go back to what they were doing after they have set the table. I know that this is a real issue for some children. They are happy playing and their parent says to them, 'Can you please come and...?' They don't want to. Quite frankly, if I am watching TV, why would I want to stop watching a programme halfway through and miss the rest of it? Try and be reasonable. If your child is doing something and says, 'But I just want to finish...', perhaps say to them, 'When you get to an appropriate place, please put the TV on hold and you will be able to come back to it later' or why not give them a warning of what they need to finish and when: 'When that programme is finished, please switch it off'. Personally I don't like other people making demands of me; I want them to consider my needs and cooperate with them, even if that means a bit of negotiation. Children want the same thing from you.

Cooperating with your children

Children think that we are not cooperating with them because:

- They have asked us to do something and we aren't listening or have not heard their request. So how do we get them to accept that we have not heard their request?

Well, we can ask our children to come and talk to us if we are in different rooms. Shouting between rooms does not make us feel like cooperating. Ask them, 'Would they shout to their teacher across the classroom?' 'No.' Well, the same rules apply at home. If your children shout between rooms ignore them until they come and find you.

The other way that would make us cooperate more with them is if they spoke to us in a less demanding way. My children do not get my attention if they say, 'I want' or forget to use the word 'please'. Keep on reminding them to use, 'Please may I have' and when they say, 'I want', say, 'Sorry but that is not how we ask for things.' The same goes for 'Please'. You can use humour to get a 'please and thank you' out of your children by saying, 'I did not hear the end of that question. Did you miss something off the end?'

- We ask them to wait while we finish doing something before giving them our attention.
- We try and put them off or get them to change their mind about something because it does not suit us. We are definitely not going to score any brownie points by doing this. For example, our children ask us to take them to the park after school. We say, 'Yes' we will. We then pick them up from school and they ask us again, 'Are we going to the park?' We say, 'No, we are going straight home'. Is this fair of us to do this? Yes, if an emergency comes up we may have to change our plans and explain why. However, if we have said that we are going to do something and then

simply decide that we actually don't want to any more is it fair to go back on our word?

- Here's another great example. How many times have you gone to the toy shop with your children to spend their birthday money and then advised them against buying something that they really want to buy because you don't like the toy or game, as it is just too messy or not what we expected them to buy. Remember that it is their money and they have the choice of how they spend it. So cooperate with them, hand over the money and let them get some pleasure out of the new game or toy. As always there is an exception to the rule and this is it: if your child wants to buy something that is not age appropriate, is dangerous or does not fall in line with your values do not let them buy it. Negotiate and persuade them to buy something else instead and give them the rationale as to why you are saying 'no'. Saying 'no' is not enough for a child to hear. They need to know the reason why.

THE TOOL TO USE

Listening and cooperation tool

1 Your child asks you to do something for them or asks for help.
2 Explain to them that you are busy and tell them what you are doing.

3 Tell them that you want to give them your undivided attention and listen to them without interruption and hear what they are saying.

4 Say to them, 'I will be able to listen to you when I have finished x and if you could just hold that thought, then you will have my full attention'.

I use that expression quite a lot, 'just hold that thought'. Alternatively, you could say to them, 'I am sorry but I am doing something else, count to 60 and I will be with you'. For example, if they want you to play games with them and you can't right at that moment then give them a time of when you can.

What is the one thing you could improve on so that your child feels that you are cooperating better with them?

The importance of rules and boundaries

Being involved in creating the rules

As parents we make up the rules. Rules for what time our children go to bed and what they should eat, do, play, etc.

We decide what these rules should be based on our own values and what we think is best for them. But have you ever wondered if your child is happy with the rules that you make and do they think that they are fair? Do they know what the rules are and why they are there? I know from experience that many children do not understand the rationale behind the rules and I think it is really important to explain to them why they are there. If they do not understand what the rule is there for they are less likely to obey it.

Rules are there to protect our children, to give them structure, order and security. All children need this and without rules they will not know what they can and cannot do. In our house we have a rule that says you must get dressed before going downstairs to play, watch TV, eat breakfast, etc. This rule was made so that:

- I could have a tidy-up upstairs while they were occupied downstairs and

- Because once they start to play or watch TV, getting dressed would then be more of a challenge.
  The rule incentivises them to get dressed first. We cooperate with each other!

There have been times when I have involved my children in creating some rules for themselves, so why don't you have a go because it can work. I asked my children what they thought the rules should be when getting ready for bed and they came up with three that I thought were useful:

- Tidy up the games and books in the lounge before going upstairs.

- Brush your teeth after your bath or shower.

- Put your dirty clothes in the laundry basket.

You can get them involved in making up rules around their pocket money, their bedroom, games, play dates, bedtime, etc. I would advise you not to have too many rules as you want your children to remember what they are. If you have a child who cannot read, draw the rules out and if they can read write them out. Either way put them on a magnetic board or the fridge.

You can also have house rules that everyone follows that have consequences. Children will love the fact that you have to follow the rules too. Why not draw up a contract that lists the rules that the whole family has to follow and if someone breaks them, even if it is you, they have to do the consequence. For example, if you do talk with your mouth full, you have to clear the table after the meal.

Discipline

You discipline according to how your parents did or from methods you have read about or seen. You may have chosen to discipline in the opposite way from your parents. Either way, you will have made up your mind about what and how you are going to do it. It is very tempting to discipline your children all the same way whatever age they are or the type of personality that they have. One punishment for all is much easier to remember. However, each child is different and so we have to administer discipline according to what they are going to respond well to.

> I recently saw a six-year-old boy who said that having time out in his bedroom was not working because he enjoyed playing with his toys and he found it very easy to get out of his bedroom if he wanted to escape. We looked together at other methods that he would respond better to. He was flattered that I had asked for his opinion and said he would prefer it if Mum and Dad did not buy him a magazine that week or let him watch TV for the rest of the day. I relayed this to his parents so they could implement it. Asking a child what they want in terms in discipline can be effective but it does depend on the child. In this case the six-year-old was very honest and wanted to have effective discipline so that he learnt right from wrong. Not all children are like that.

Discipline has to work, otherwise a child is never going to learn how to behave in the way you would like them to. Discipline reinforces the boundaries that children should already be aware of and it should prevent the need for punishment. Discipline, taught in a loving and considerate way, encourages children to behave well. Punishment, on the other hand, is seen as negative as you are taking away something from the child that they value. You are much more likely to get a stronger reaction, such as kicking, screaming or shouting when you punish a child than when you discipline.

When I mention discipline and punishment here it is because it is possible to get the input from your child. Children know what works for them and actually love and embrace the rules and boundaries that you impose on them even though they would never tell you that. They know that they do not like to be grounded or not allowed on the PlayStation for a week. I have seen children who say the punishment does not work because it does not bother them to have something taken away from them. They have actually verbalised that they would prefer a punishment that would 'hurt' them.

If you asked your child what punishment they would like, what would they say?

For some children punishments just do not work but rewards do. Only you know your child and what they respond best to. If your child prefers to be rewarded, and I am sure most do, I see no harm in asking them how they want to be motivated. Do they want stickers or time with you, do they want to choose what they have for dinner, get a magazine, want to stay up late or do they want to watch their favourite TV programme that day? Whatever they say, within reason, go with it. I have had lots of children say to me, 'Why doesn't Mum do this instead of this?' and the suggestions that they give are not unreasonable. They are generally about Mum or Dad treating them a certain way. If you are finding it hard to motivate your child then discuss with them how they would like to be motivated to behave in the manner that you would like them to.

Discipline and punishments provide boundaries. Without boundaries there are no consequences and children need to learn about adhering to rules because they are everywhere – not just in childhood but when they enter the working environment. Boundaries are the foundation for raising well-mannered, confident children who know what acceptable behaviour is and what it is not.

Effective 'cooperation' language

A child will come into my clinic and say, 'My mum won't listen to me. I would like her to listen to what I have to say and maybe think about why I want to do something. Because she won't listen I have to shout to be heard.'

In order to get the attention of their parents, children will first use a normal voice to ask for what they want and then, if they still feel they are not being heard by their parents, they will put their voice up a gear in attitude and volume. Some children won't directly ask their parents to cooperate with them more, they will shout their need or they will behave in an adverse way to get their attention. I remember years ago working with a girl who said her mum did not listen to her. The girl would slam doors and shout to get her mum to cooperate and listen to her. Shouting and slamming doors is disrespectful. If you can teach your children to talk to you in a humane way then they will treat others with respect.

Teach your child how to communicate effectively

Teaching cooperation is a long-term investment. When your children are young they are more likely to listen and cooperate with you as you are their parent. Once they reach their teenage years they are more likely to challenge your authority and not want to comply when you ask them to do something. However, if we constantly pull the hierarchy card – 'Do this because I am the parent' – our children may not be able to assert themselves later on in life and expect to be told what to do all the time. They will either lose their voice to speak up or resent adults for bossing them about.

If you show children how you can communicate effectively and give them your time – easier said than done sometimes – then you can start listening to their needs and wishes and show them that you are willing to cooperate in a civil and orderly way. As I mentioned in an earlier chapter, communicating effectively is about taking time to listen to your children and showing you are interested in what they are saying.

You can also negotiate with them when they need your help with something. For example, when my son asks me to help him tie his shoes I say, 'Yes', if he can then wait by the door so we can go out. He thinks that if I tie his shoe-laces he can go back inside to play afterwards. What I want is for him to wait by the front door so I negotiate with him: 'I will do up your shoes if you can wait by the door when I have finished.' The instruction is very clear and there is no reason for him not to cooperate.

Parents, you can make life easier for yourselves. Children generally respond well to negotiation, so give them some.

THE TOOL TO USE

How to ask tool

Children don't cooperate well when they are being ordered about or rushed by their parents. If you order your child about they will stick their heels in and take longer to do the thing you asked or not do it at all. Your child will also complain about the 'order'.

1 Before you open your mouth to ask your children to do something, think about what you are going to say.

2 How are you going to say it?

3 Think about their response to the way you are going to ask them to do something. Ask yourself: Would I like to be asked in this way?

4 Is how you ask them going to put them in a bad mood or will they be agreeable to the request?

Ask your child; don't give orders

If we ask they will cooperate; if we demand they will put up a fight. For example, let's say you would like your children to tidy up the lounge at the end of each day. Rather than ordering them to do it – *'Boys tidy the lounge'* – you could say, 'Boys could you tidy the lounge please so we can go upstairs and start getting ready for bed/read some stories/do something together.' One of the ways you can motivate your children to tidy up is to use the faithful stopwatch and challenge them to tidy up in a certain time or tidy up all together, with each person responsible for tidying away certain items. This makes the job in hand fair and it shows your children that you are happy to get involved and help tidy up. Your child will also receive the message that they are part of a team working towards the same goal.

Children like to feel they are respected and will cooperate more if they feel the value, so ask them what they would like to tidy up in the lounge first or how many minutes you should set the stopwatch for.

What motivates your child to be cooperative?

Apart from bribery and rewards, is there another way for your children to cooperate with you? Yes there is. You can negotiate, as mentioned before, you can use humour or you can play a game to get them to do what you would like them to do. An example of game playing is the journey to school with my children. When we arrive at the school we get out of the car and walk down the hill to the gate. On the way we play the game where you are not allowed to step on a crack. If you step on a crack you lose a life and you only have three lives. I lose most of my lives every day and I know my children do too, but who cares? The game gets us to our destination and it keeps the journey lively and fun.

Children are naturally open to be motivated by rewards and will be more cooperative when these are used. Rewarding children can be a great way to teach them that they have to be prepared to work towards something that they want while we get the behaviour we desire.

What motivates your child to be cooperative?

Expressing your appreciation

Paying attention and expressing your appreciation to your children for not only complying with your request but doing it in a cooperative manner will impact upon them in a way that makes them feel good about themselves. They will be inspired to continue in a cooperative manner as they remember how they like feeling being a positive part of what happens in their home and in their family. Say thank you and be specific about their behaviour: 'The way you did that was amazing. Helping out has made life easier for me and we have saved time, so thank you for your help.'

Children want to feel a sense of belonging. When they choose to act in a way that contributes to the well-being of the family atmosphere they gain a sense of pride. They are proud of themselves for making a positive contribution!

Checklist

- Cooperation does not mean giving in to your child.
- There are ways of getting your child to do what you want.
- Children can have input into rules and boundaries.
- Discipline reinforces the boundaries.
- Use the right language to get your child to cooperate with you.
- Know what motivates your child.

chapter four

How to help your child handle their emotions

'When dealing with people, remember you are not dealing with creatures of logic, but with creatures of emotion, creatures bristling with prejudice, and motivated by pride and vanity'

DALE CARNEGIE

It is not easy for children to understand their feelings. One of the reasons that they don't understand them is because they have so many feelings and some of them feel similar to others. It is easy for children to get them mixed up. I cannot tell you how many times a child has said to me that they are sad when what they really mean is that they are upset or they say they are angry when in fact they are frustrated.

Children can also go from being really happy to really upset, or really upset to happy, in a matter of minutes and feelings can hang around in their bodies for a long period of time. We know that because when a child gets angry they can stay angry for ages and when they are having a great experience they will remain happy for a while.

How to teach your child to recognise their feelings

It is important for children to recognise their feelings so that they can verbalise them correctly and deal with them in an appropriate way. If a child is feeling angry then they need to recognise the anger so that they can either stop it before it starts or they know how to control it before they do something they may regret. Anger is a valid feeling, it just needs to be appropriately expressed so no one gets hurt.

When children are happy there is less, or even nothing, to worry about. They feel happy and there are no consequences apart from perhaps annoying others around them who do not share their zest for life.

One thing that is important about feelings is that it is essential for us to teach our children to be able to read other people's feelings so they react towards them in the right way. They need to be compassionate or sympathetic when they see another child looking upset. If they see a child who looks angry then perhaps they know to stay away from that child until they have calmed down.

What we would like for our children is for them to be able to acknowledge their feelings rather than suppress them. There are many thoughts and beliefs behind their feelings and if we want or need to tackle those thoughts and beliefs we need to know how the child feels. For example, a child may feel scared of the dark because they believe that bad things happen in the dark or a child may feel worried about their mum going out at night because they think that she will not come home. What you can do to get the feeling out is to talk about how they feel and what their belief is behind it.

THE TOOL TO USE

Feelings tool

Talk to your child about the way they feel and challenge their beliefs behind the feeling. Children and adults alike hold irrational beliefs about themselves and the world around them. If you challenge them they can hopefully change the way they feel and eradicate the belief.

You ask them: 'How do you feel?'

Child: 'Worried.'

You: 'What makes you worried?'

Child: 'When you are late for me when school ends.'

You: 'What does it mean if I am late?'

Child: 'It means you have something better to do.'

The belief for the child here is that they are not worth you being on time to pick them up from school.

What can you do if your child confuses their feelings?

There are two easy exercises you can do with your child if they do not recognise their feelings easily. The first one is to talk with them about how different emotions feel. What would your child say being happy feels like, or anxious, sad, hurt or lonely? What would their body and face look like when they feel these things? By talking about how feelings feel your child can familiarise themselves with the changes in emotion that they have. It may also help them with how other people are feeling. If they see a friend who looks lonely they can ask them if they are all right or ask them if they want to join in a game.

The second exercise you can do with your child is to get them to match up their feelings to different situations and people. You start by listing out the prominent people in their life and the situations that they find themselves in regularly and write them down on the left-hand side of a piece of paper. Then on the right-hand side list some feelings that children can identify with. Once you have written these feelings down ask your child to match up a feeling with each person in their life and match up a feeling to each situation by drawing a line connecting them. There can be more than one feeling to each person or situation. This exercise can be quite difficult for some children so you may need to provide some help.

MATCHING UP DIFFERENT SITUATIONS AND PEOPLE WITH FEELINGS

Mum		Clever
	Calm	Great
Dad		Challenged
	Happy	Useless
Sister		
Brother		Upset
	Angry	Shy
Teachers		Excited
	Sad	Exciting
Sue (friend)		Frustrated
Lily (friend)	Jealous	Worried
Jane (friend)		Nervous
	Scared	Bored
School		Anxious
	Relaxed	Unhappy
Home		Annoyed
Karate club	Lonely	Frightened
Playground		Wonderful

The exercise can really make your child think and separate out what feeling goes where in their life and with whom. It also provides a great starting point for you to talk about why they feel what they do when they are with friends, family or outside of the home environment. This is where your coaching 'chat' can start.

How could you get your child to open up more about their feelings?

Acknowledgement of good feelings

I saw Asher, aged eight, who would never show his friends or family how he was feeling. His parents wanted me to work with Asher to help him express himself verbally, but also teach him how he could let others know how he was feeling by his facial expressions. When I met him I could tell he was not one of those excitable types who would jump up and down when something fantastic happened. I also realised that when he did acknowledge a good feeling he would do so quietly and his expression would not change. We talked about feelings together and I explained that showing someone we are happy, excited or enthusiastic is important for the other person, as it makes them feel appreciated or that you want them to join in your achievement. Sharing feelings is important in friendships as it builds trust. If we can't show our feelings to our friends then we are saying to them that we do not trust them with our feelings. Asher and I spent time talking about feelings and pulling faces – each face had a feeling behind it. That was probably one of my best sessions! After our session Asher went off and practised his expressions. When I spoke to his mum midweek she said that he was trying really hard to convey how he felt using his face and that he was slowly starting to talk about his feelings when she asked him about school.

We need to teach children to acknowledge their good feelings so they can share them with other people. Attitude breeds attitude, and therefore if your child is happy others around them will also be. The same goes for if they are unhappy. Rather than keep unhappy or bad feelings inside themselves to fester away they should share them. Festering makes bad feelings feel worse. Opening up about their feelings shows vulnerability but it can also take the burden off your child. They say a problem shared is a problem halved and to some extent it is true. If a child shows that they are unhappy about something then they can start working towards a situation where they can be happier.

Knowing you are loved is also a good feeling. Occasionally a child will tell me that they do not feel loved. This can be because they have low self-esteem. If your child says they do not feel loved why not talk about all of the things that you do for them and that each thing you do shows them that you love them. It can be as simple as you asking what they want for dinner. You care enough to ask. Or it could be that you buy their favourite biscuits.

Acknowledgement of 'other' feelings

It is not good for children to keep some 'other' feelings inside. 'Other' feelings need to be shared and some need to be resolved.

For example, according to his parents, Tim was very unhappy. They did not know why so Tim and I had a chat about his life. We identified that he was unhappy with the way school was going. He was putting loads of effort into his work but not getting the grades he expected. He was disappointed in himself and could not see how he was going to improve in his school work. Tim was festering and not talking about it to anyone. Once he did open up and tell me what was going on he felt relieved. After looking at what he could do to stop feeling like this he went and spoke to his teacher, who was able to point out what he could do to increase the standard of his work. He had just needed an extra boost of confidence to talk to his teacher and tell him how he felt. Once he did the problem was resolved.

There are lots of 'other' feelings that children have and as parents we want to be able to walk our children through them and get them through to the other side. I have decided to address the feelings that are the most common, where parents feel that their children could do with a little bit of help. So let's look together at each one, find ways of how we can talk to our children about them and turn their unhappy feelings into happier ones.

Handling anger

Children get angry and there are lots of different reasons why. Common causes include friends letting them down, parents not allowing them to do something, brothers and sisters being annoying, being treated unfairly or when something does not go to plan. They can also get angry when there is a conflict over possessions – one person wants something the other one has or it could be that someone is teasing them and they don't like it and that person is pushing their buttons too far. Children can also become angry if they are pushed or shoved regardless of the reason, if they are rejected from a group of peers or if they are asked to do something that they do not want to do. Children are not great at managing their anger and therefore need some help with controlling and channelling it.

Being angry shows passion and determination as well as being a natural response when we need to defend ourselves or warn others not to take advantage of us. Children find it tough to own the anger and once the anger has owned them other people can get emotionally and physically hurt through the awful words that they say and their actions. The children I see do not like to get angry mainly because they do not like how it makes them feel and also because of the consequences it can bring. If they lash out or kick or throw an object they can be grounded or punished.

Find the cause of the anger

If your child has an anger problem it is important to find out what makes them angry. It is important to let them know that it is okay to feel angry but they have to take responsibility for it. It is easy for your child to say, 'Well they make me angry', because someone has said something that they don't agree with, but what exactly made them angry and what can they do to stop the anger from starting? We can teach our children that they have control over their response and they can choose to be angry or they can accept what another person is saying or doing.

Claire's sister, Natalie would make her angry by annoying her – saying silly things. Claire would shout at her younger sister. Natalie would slam the door. Claire would cry to her mum and get cross with her for not listening or taking her seriously. Claire's mum would get cross and would put Claire in her bedroom. How would Claire like to change the situation? Claire said that at the point of telling Mum that Natalie had annoyed her, rather than get upset, Mum should suggest she went to her room to calm down. I discussed this with Claire's mum and she began to help Claire with her suggestion. While Claire put this into action, I worked with Claire on how better she could respond to her

sister so that she did not evoke a reaction when provoked,
although this was a much longer process to implement.

How to help your child combat their anger

If your child feels that they cannot change the situation
and finds themselves getting angry, do they have the power
to stop it before it gets out of control – in other words, can
they recognise what is happening in their body? If children
recognise the physiological changes in their body they will
know what is going to happen next and then take alternative action. Do their hands clench or do they feel their
heart beating faster? Can they feel themselves getting
redder? Can your child reflect back and see what the
trigger is – what makes them see red? Ask them what they
notice about their body. Noticing the physical changes in
their body is the first stage of combatting anger.

The next step is called 'changing my attitude'. By this I
mean your child changes their attitude about what someone
is saying or doing to them that irritates them and just lets
it go over their head. For example, if someone says something horrible to them can they just think to themselves, 'I
don't know why they said that but they are wrong. They
don't deserve a reaction.'

Or perhaps they could accept that they have to do
something they don't want to do when someone makes a
request of them? For instance, when you ask them to lay
the table, why don't they think, 'It's not worth getting

angry or upset about doing it. I will just do it instead of making a fuss.' Suggest to them that they will have to do it anyway and by getting angry about it the job will take much longer.

If your child does not feel they are able to do either of the above, then perhaps they could recognise the anger and release it in a safe way that is not going to hurt anyone else – verbally or physically.

They could do this by verbalising their angry feelings to the person they are with. They may not want the person's help but if they said to them out loud, 'I am angry right now', they can both acknowledge how one of them feels. Would they prefer to say, 'I am feeling really angry and I just need to go and let off some steam?' or 'Please do not talk to me when I feel this angry, it may make it worse' or 'I need to be by myself as I can feel myself getting angry.' Are they able to say this to their friends or do they feel more comfortable saying it to their family? Many of the children I see say they are happy to say they are angry at home but not with friends. With their friends they would rather run away and get rid of their anger alone somewhere else.

Once they have walked away and are alone what could they do? Would doing something physical help or would they prefer to do something relaxing to calm down? I think it is easier if we look at how your child can diffuse their anger in both the school and home setting because different tools will be required for both.

School

In the school setting children could:

- Kick a ball.
- Find some quiet space.
- Talk to themselves to calm down by saying, 'Be calm, don't react' or 'Breathe'.
- Count to 20 backwards.
- Recite the word 'relax' over and over again.
- Take deep breaths.
- Go and have a drink of water.
- Talk to a teacher who is not involved in the situation.
- Try and find a funny side to the situation.
- Say to themselves, 'I will not let them make me angry, I am a good person, I will be fine.'
- Stop and see the bigger picture. Perhaps they could think why that person is trying to wind them up? It is possible the other person is angry about something else but is taking it out on them.

Whichever option they decide to take will mean them walking away from the situation. One of the children I saw who had anger issues decided she was going to go inside the school building and find a quiet place to write down her thoughts to get rid of her anger. I asked her if she was allowed to go into the school during break times and she said it would be okay. Children have to do what is right for them.

One of my favourite ways to get rid of anger is to put it in a tray or drawer. If your child gets angry at school they can pretend to put their anger in their tray and leave it there so they don't come out of school and take it out on you. They can talk about the anger so long as the emotions and feelings stay in the tray.

> *I had a client, a child called Ella, who tried out this idea and it really worked for her. Ella would put any of her 'other' feelings in the drawer so that they stayed at school and she did not take them home with her.*

Home

The home environment is so different when it comes to letting go of anger because there is more space, other places to go and options available:

- If you have a back garden and it is not raining too hard, your child can go and kick a ball about, shoot a few baskets or just run around the garden getting rid of their pent-up anger.
- They could shout out their anger in their bedroom or outside in the garden.
- Shake the anger out of their body.
- Listen to music.
- Play a computer game if it will calm them down or get them to re-focus on something else. (For some children computer games can make anger symptoms worse.)

- Lie on their bed and think. If a child has done something wrong being in their own room with space to think will give them time to work out what happened, what was the trigger for them getting angry and what they need to do to get life back on track.

- Watch TV if the programme is of a relaxing nature.

- Tell Mum, Dad or their siblings that they need to be on their own to calm down and when they are they will come back, talk about it and apologise if necessary.

- Have an angry drawer or a secret place to store anger like Ella.

- Go to their room and take their anger out on their pillow.

- Play their musical instrument loudly to get rid of their negative feelings.

If you have a child who likes to write things down why not suggest to them that they keep an anger diary where they can write down their thoughts, what made them angry, how did they deal with it, was it successful, what would they do next time? They can write or draw in the diary too. The diary can highlight beliefs that the child has as well as their thoughts. If they shared this with you, you would be able to challenge some of those beliefs.

To help control their anger they can also get involved in other activities outside of the home; yoga, martial arts and dance are all ways of channelling anger.

How do you currently help your child with their anger? What ideas would you try out with them?

Children need to understand that when they are angry it is not the fault of another person; they are responsible for their own actions and emotions. Someone can make them feel really angry, what they must not do is hit back.

Being afraid and/or scared

It is common for children to be afraid – afraid of the dark, new situations, fear of falling, bugs, loud machines or natural disasters. The fear makes sense to a child who has not had the experience or knowledge to know better and they often need us to help them to overcome the fear and make it more rational. Fear is also a natural response for a child who has experienced some kind of misfortune such as a bereavement or car accident. Often when our child expresses their fears to us we don't take them seriously – we sometimes ignore it and hope it will go away in time or we tease them about it. Either way it can make the child's fear worse. Children need us to talk about it. If it is shoved under the carpet it can lead a child to have anxiety and panic attacks in later years. We need to discuss with our child the reality of the fear and explain to them that we can get scared of new things or certain circumstances. Share with them how you tackle your fears. Perhaps make them see that you are human and let them get involved in helping you overcome one of your fears. For example, if you are afraid of spiders show them how brave you are by taking a spider out of the house.

When it comes to new situations take the time to reassure your child that these situations can be exciting and eventful. Show them that you are unafraid and calm in new situations and if they are worried about events that occur outside of a person's control try and put them into perspective. My oldest child became afraid of natural disasters when he was six years old. They had been discussing them in class around the time of the tsunami and earthquakes in Japan and he thought that every time it rained heavily there would be a flood. He had so many questions about earthquakes, floods and tsunamis and we kept on answering them at the same time as telling him why this would not happen in the UK. I still provide a lot of reassurance to him now a year on.

There can be no logic when it comes to being afraid.

> *I remember working with a girl called Lily who was worried about a hole in the pavement outside her house. She was afraid she would fall down it and it would swallow her up.*
>
> *I asked her, 'How big is it?'*
>
> *Lily: 'The size of a tennis ball.'*
>
> *Me: 'How big are you? Could you fit into a hole that size?'*
>
> *Lily: 'No.'*
>
> *Me: 'If you cannot fit down it, could it still swallow you up?*
>
> *Lily: 'No.'*
>
> *I got a ball and asked her to push it through a circle I had made with my hands. She saw it was impossible to do and realised that she should no longer be afraid. When I asked her about the hole in the next coaching session she said she was no longer worried about it. She had looked at the hole again and realised just how small it really was.*

Excessive worries

We worry and children worry. What can you do when they have a worry? Well, you need to get them to change their thinking. What are they worrying about? What are the possibilities of that happening? Is there anything good in the thing they are worrying about? How else could they think? What is the worst that can happen?

One example of worrying is about the son of a friend of mine, Henry. He is a natural worrier and gets upset easily when it comes to new situations. It can be easy as seeing a 3D film or leaving him with a mum of one of her friends whom he has not been to before. My friend has found it hard work getting Henry to embrace new situations. She came to me for help when she realised he would have to get used to them more as her new job determined he would have to be left with friends sometimes.

I spent a session with Henry and I asked him these questions:

I asked him, 'Why don't you like going to a friend's house after school?'

Henry: 'Because I prefer to be at home.'

Me: 'Why do you prefer to be at home?'

Henry: 'Because I worry about being at my friends.'

Me: 'What do you worry about?'

Henry: 'That I won't have anything to do or it won't be fun.'

Me: 'Is that a possibility?'

Henry: 'Yes.'

Me: 'Why?'

Henry: 'Some of my friends don't like to do the same things as me.'

Me, 'What about if you agreed on what you were going to do before you went to their house. Would that stop the worrying?'

Henry: 'Maybe.'

Me: 'Okay, so do we have a plan? If you decide on the activities you will do at your friend's house you will be happier and not worry?'

Henry: 'I think so.'

Me: 'Okay, so let's try it out!'

Henry said if his mum took him into the house and got him interested in an activity he enjoyed he would find it easier and not worry so much.

There are many children that do not like to be left with a babysitter or with another person for a period of time. If your child does not like to be left give them a time of when you will return or give them a stopwatch so they can count down the minutes. The stopwatch idea only works if you are leaving them during the day and for a short period of time. Keep to your side of the bargain, though, otherwise you will have a very upset child.

Many children do not like being left completely alone.

Skye, aged 14, didn't. Skye had to come home to an empty house while her mum was on her way home from work. She had about 20 minutes on her own at home and would feel sad and lonely not knowing what to do with herself. Did she have to come home on her own? Yes. Did she have to feel that way? No. What could she do that would keep her busy and possibly enjoy the time on her own. She suggested she could get herself a drink, find something to eat and listen to some music while she waited for Mum. The next day she tried it out and was much happier and the 20 minutes flew by.

If you have a child who does not like being left alone why not arrange for a friend to come and keep them company or they go to a friend's house? Alternatively, ask your child what could they do to make the most of the time they had on their own?

Once children start school they are more aware of life around them. They learn about the world's goings on, they hear things from their friends and they see the news. Whatever worries your child has ask them to write them down and challenge their thoughts. How likely is it that a bomb will go off in their town? What would make them feel more secure in their thoughts? Talk to them about reality and that bombings, earthquakes and riots are not the norm.

Frustration

Children want to get it right; they can't. They want you to listen; you don't. They want others to behave in a certain way; they won't. All of these can create frustration. How can you help your frustrated child? You can do this by getting them to take deep breaths and realise that they cannot change other people and that they are only responsible for themselves. If they are frustrated because of themselves then break down exactly what is making them feel that way and talk them through the activity or challenge they are trying so that they approach it in a more relaxed way. For example, if they are frustrated doing their homework break it down into bite-sized chunks with them and talk through the parts that they are finding hard.

If your child is getting frustrated when they are trying to talk to you and they seem to think you are not listening, it is a good idea to get them to calm down, especially if the frustration has got to the point of aggressive behaviour. Be the adult here and teach them that you will not listen to them when they make demands.

Being angry, afraid, worrying or frustrated can make children feel stressed so it is important that they know how to manage it.

Stress management

Stress is normal for everyone and hopefully as adults we know how to deal with it in a healthy way. Children, on the other hand, may not and may need a helping hand. My children manifest their stress by shouting (very loudly) and not making much sense in their shouting (almost the same as frustration). My first reaction is to calm them down and ask them to speak to me in a respectful way, clearly and as calmly as they can and listen, listen, listen.

Stress can do strange things to your body. Lots of children say that they feel stressed and don't know what to do about it. I talk to them about exercise, relaxation and diet. I have a qualification in nutrition so that comes in fairly handy sometimes. Stress is shown in the following ways and children need to recognise that if they have any of these signs it is time to destress: not sleeping, headaches or stomachaches, not wanting to speak to anyone, hiding their feelings, getting angry or short-tempered, being moody or biting their nails. Stress can manifest itself in many different ways and only you know your child well enough to recognise it.

Help me to de-stress and relax

Children have such busy lives – school, after school clubs, play dates, weekend activities, etc. It is good for them to be active but they also need down time to unwind, relax, process their thoughts and feelings, clear their minds of all the hustle and bustle of daily life and let their bodies have a rest. It's just as important to their mental health as eating well, sleeping well and exercising. Have you ever asked your child if they feel that they are doing too much and can you tell if they are not coping with life's demands?

I saw Jane about a year ago and she was unhappy with the demands that were being made of her. She had not let on to her parents that she was unhappy as she did not want to upset them. She was finding it hard to fit everything in – her homework, the after school activities and seeing her friends. Jane was also finding it hard to sleep at night. Together, Jane and I looked at her schedule for the week and talked about the activities she was doing. Did she enjoy doing all of them? No, she wanted to drop two of them. Did she think her mum would let her drop them? She was not sure so we made a note of them to discuss with her mum. We then looked at when she was doing her homework. She was doing a bit here and a bit there. If she dropped those two activities she would then have two block periods in the week when she could do her homework instead of having to squeeze it in between activities. Jane also felt that she was not getting to see her friends as much as she wanted so we looked at when she could do that. I asked her, 'How important is it for you to see your friends – once or twice a week or once a month?' She thought once a week would make her feel happier and she could see her friends at her house or at theirs. In fact she came up with a great idea. Sometimes she thought she could study with her friends then she could see them and get her homework done.

After speaking to her mum and discussing the actions Jane wanted to implement, her mum let her drop one of the after school activities. This took some pressure off Jane and it gave her a bit more time to herself to either do her homework or see her friends.

I had hoped that doing less would mean Jane had less on her mind and help her get to bed earlier and sleep better. But even with the new routine, she still seemed a bit stressed so I asked her if she wanted to learn some relaxation techniques. She thought it was a good idea. I talked her through the relaxation techniques below.

I think relaxation techniques can really help children de-stress and clear their minds. All of the relaxation techniques can be done sitting or lying somewhere quiet and warm where your child, or you and your child, if you are going to do the relaxation together, will not be interrupted.

THE TOOL TO USE

De-stress tool

1 Ask your child to lie still on a flat surface – a bed, couch or the floor.

2 Get them to focus on different muscles of the body and try relaxing them one at a time.

3 Start by getting them to wiggle their fingers, shake out their hands and stretch their arms.

4 Next, get them to tense and relax all parts of their body. They can tense their toes for 10 seconds and then relax, and then move on to their legs, buttocks, stomach and moving up the body – tensing and relaxing each part. They could also work from the head down to the toes. When the whole body has been tensed they can just lie still and relax.

As they do this exercise your child will hopefully be so focused on a part of their body that they won't be thinking about anything else. In a quiet room, this can really help their mind to relax. Once you have taught your child to do this they will be able to do it by themselves. If your child does not like to be in complete silence then perhaps they could put some relaxing music on at the same time.

Deep breathing

Teach your child to take a deep breath, hold it for about five seconds and then release it. As they exhale get them to say the word 'relax' to themselves. Deep breaths will help them relax because they are concentrating on what they are doing and the word 'relax' will remind them of what they need to do. After a few deep breaths they should feel relaxed.

Visualisation

Get your child to shut their eyes and imagine that they are somewhere they love. It could be the beach or the fairground. It could be a quiet place or a noisy one. They could be with friends or family. With their eyes closed they can transport themselves to that setting and imagine the sounds, colours and the smells of that special spot. The thoughts and imagery of such a positive picture in their mind will help them feel relaxed. I often think of lying on the beach thinking of the seagulls crying and my children making sandcastles and laughing as they splash in the sea. There is nothing like a free holiday!

If you have a child who does not do well at lying still or have the concentration for relaxation exercises then maybe you could look at more physical exercise such as running, kicking a ball around or shooting some goals. All these ways can get rid of 'other' feelings.

There are also other ways that you can suggest to your child to relax:

- Listening to music, reading, watching television. They can listen to music, especially calming and gentle music, as it can take their mind to different places away from the stress of reality. The same can be said for reading and watching TV. They can be great ways for a child to unwind their thoughts and their feelings. TV can be real escapism.
- Laughing. Laughing is an excellent relaxation technique for children. We all like to laugh, don't we? Get your child involved in making up silly jokes or watch something funny like YouTube clips. Laughing relaxes most of the muscles of the face and gets them to focus on the less serious parts of life.

What does your child do to relax?

Importance of sleep and good nutrition

It is extremely important that a child sleeps well, as it can really affect their well-being if they don't. When chatting to a child I will ask how much sleep they are getting if they seem stressed. If they aren't getting enough or they find it hard to drop off at night we will talk about relaxation techniques and/or keeping a journal. The reason most children find it difficult to sleep is because they are worried about something. If they write it down, the worry stays on the paper and they are worry-free to go to sleep. I have mentioned journals several times before but I do believe they can help. They can even help you if *you* can't sleep because you are worried about your children!

Checklist

- Children can mix up their feelings.
- Beliefs and thoughts are behind their feelings.
- Good and 'other' feelings should be shared.
- Help your child notice the telltale signs of getting angry.
- Rationalise their worries and fears.
- Relaxation and imagery can help children to de-stress.

chapter five

How to help your child with friendships

'True happiness consists not in the multitude of friends, but in their worth and choice' SAMUEL JOHNSON

Not all children find friendships easy. Some children don't have the confidence to make new friends and others make friends easily but then find it difficult to keep them. Some children, when there is an upset between themselves and their friends, do not know how to solve the issue and get the friendship back on track. Friendships can be complex as they involve a multitude of personalities and every friend your child has will have their own wants and needs. It is likely your child is going to have things in common with their friends, perhaps they dress similar, but they will think and act differently from them when they are in the same situation.

I find that children need to be team players when it comes to friendships – know when to take the lead and when to drop back, know when to negotiate and when to back down. Children need to have certain attributes to make them work. Friendships require a lot of hard work, understanding and patience.

I think children can start to find friendships difficult once they enter into the world of education. At nursery school they take the other children at face value. They just get on and play with the other children and if someone is unkind to them I don't think the child worries too much about it. But once children start primary school they are suddenly exposed to many different personalities and they can find it difficult to adapt. Nursery provides a shelter to them where they have not had to sort out their differences with other children. At nursery if they did not get on with another child they were just separated or told to apologise and forget about the incident.

There can be many strong characters at primary school and that can be intimidating to a child who has had a small social circle until now. There are children who don't know how to share or play nicely and it can take time for younger children to find their feet and seek out like-minded children who share similar characteristics. Even when they do find like-minded peers are they really prepared to deal with the children who have strong characters?

Why do some children have friendship problems?

Here are a few reasons why children have problems with friendships:

- They have low self-esteem and low self-belief.
- They read into situations that are not necessarily there.
- They are shy or would prefer to be alone.
- They have physical, mental or emotional differences to their peers.

The importance of friendships

All children need friends. They need them to play with, explore new situations, share, be creative with and learn from. They are also important in helping children develop emotionally and socially as through interaction children learn the importance of social skills such as manners and etiquette. All children need a friend for those troubling and transitional times. A friendly face can support them when faced with life changes – moving to a new school or moving areas, going through puberty, family breakdowns, disappointments, etc.

Friendships teach children how other children their age think and feel and they can also learn that different people in the same situation react in different ways. For example, a child who is pushed over by someone may run to the teacher and tell, whereas another child may dust themselves down and walk away. Children learn a great deal about themselves, too, in friendships, as they compare themselves to their peers – their physical traits, their interests, their passions and strengths. They realise what they are good at or not so good at and what makes them unique.

As well as the social and emotional factors, friendships are necessary for healthy psychological development. Research shows that children with friends have a greater sense of well-being, better self-esteem and fewer social problems as adults than individuals without friends. That is why it is so important that you navigate with your child the problems they have with friendships when they are young. It is not nice falling out with friends. Aside from the help you can give your child with their self-esteem, I think friendship is an area where your child can really benefit from your input.

Making friends

As I said earlier, many children do not find it easy making new friends but there are strategies you can help your child with if they say they don't have any friends. This may or may not be true but it is your job to find out. When I work with a child who says that they don't have any friends we look at why they think that. Firstly, is it really true that they have no friends, and secondly, what have they done to make friends and have they given it a long enough time? Friendships take time to develop and you need to explain this to them. It takes time to get to know other people and to be able to trust them with your feelings and thoughts.

I worked with Emma, aged seven, who said she had tried to make friends with a group of girls but they did not seem interested in making friends with her. When she was in the playground she would stand next to her peers and listen into their conversation. She did not voluntarily join in with what they were talking about. I asked her why she thought they were not including her in the conversation. Perhaps they thought she was just happy to listen in and did not want to add anything into the conversation. Maybe she wasn't making a big enough effort to say something. After discussing the value of friendships and what they entail, Emma felt that she would have to push herself forward and join in the chat, otherwise they were never going to get to know her and trust her enough to bring her into the group. The next time she saw them in the playground she was going to go over, chip into their conversation and see what happened. She did and the girls listened to her. She asked if she could play a game with them and all was fine. Her feelings of loneliness diminished and she was now able to say she had friends.

Teaching your child how to make friends

If your child wants you to help them with making friends you could use the following strategies:

- Ask them, 'Which children do they like the look of at school?' If they had to choose two children who would they be? Why? How would they start a conversation with them?

My suggestion is that they use questions that start with the words 'what', 'why', 'where' and 'when', as they all allow for a conversation to start up.

> *I used this tactic with Tamsin. She tried it out for a week when she started her new school and it worked. The four 'w' questions gave her answers to things she wanted to know about the other girls and she felt that she had started building the foundations for new friendships.*

- You could teach your child to interact with their peers while playing alongside them. For example, while they are playing next to them they could talk about what they are doing or talk about things that have happened to them recently. Why not role-play this out with them – you could pretend to be the friend.

- You could talk to your child about the importance of showing an interest in what other people are doing and saying. Explain to them that it makes other people feel special and it can be done by asking potential friends questions. If they find it hard to do then practise asking simple questions with them like, 'What did you do last night?' or give them a compliment like, 'I really like your ... where did you get it from?' There are lots of questions they can ask. Asking questions is a great way to get to know other people.

- You could teach your child how to pay more attention to others. There are words and signs that you can teach your child that show other people you are paying attention to their conversation, 'um', 'yes', 'great', really' are just a few. Practise with your child if they need to grasp the level of interaction needed to show they are interested in what others are saying.

- You could suggest to your child that they invite some friends over to your house after school or at the weekend. Your child should feel much more relaxed being in their own environment and find it easier to chat and discover what their friends like doing.

- You could discuss the traits that you know are necessary in friendships that make them run more smoothly. Do you perceive your child to have the following – patience, understanding, dependability, compromising, loyalty, trustworthiness, ability to share, helpfulness, acceptance of others' mistakes, good listening skills. If not perhaps you could help them gain these traits by discussing them in detail.

- Ask your child if they think are giving out the right signals that they want to be friends with someone. Are they smiling, using good eye contact and relaxed body language? Are they being friendly? Do they help others if they need help? Are they talking kindly about their friends to other friends? Are they respecting others' property and opinions? Are they making an effort to talk and to share? All of the above encourage friendships to happen. If your child is not putting out these signals then you can help them practise smiling, eye contact, using good body language, etc. The best way to do this is by acting it out together – kind of role-playing. Have a conversation with them and encourage them to use the right signals. Regarding the interpersonal skills needed for friendships, ask them what they look for in a friend and are they being that person themselves.

- Do you know if your child is making friends with people who are the same and different to them? It can be interesting for your child to be with people who are different to them so that they can learn about other cultures, families, etc.

- If your child wants to make new friends and does not know who to become friends with they should look around and see who is like them just by observation. It may be that someone in their class has shown an interest in music and your child also likes music. It is much easier to make conversation with someone who shares the same interest. Who do they like the look of, who is friendly to them and who does not look threatening?

- Encourage your child to have lots of friends rather than one best friend. This will mean they will always have someone to play and talk with in the playground. Whatever you do don't force them to play with children you choose for them to be friends with. Your child may not enjoy their time being with that person and possibly make the time awkward so it doesn't happen again. Your child has to make their own friends and, with a little support from you, they will.

- If you are worried that your child is not making lots of new friends and only has a handful of friends, ask them if they are happy. They may like to have fewer quality friendships rather than having lots of friends and acquaintances. It also seems to be that older children tend to gravitate towards having fewer but closer friends. Accept that this is their choice.

- Talk to your child about the obstacles to friendships that they have by sitting down with them and discussing each one and then finding a solution to each obstacle. For example, it may be that your child wants to be friends with someone who plays football and they don't like playing football. They then have a choice to make – do they play football even though they hate it or do they find someone else to play with? Your child can still be friends with someone who plays football at school – they can see them outside of school.

I am confident that these strategies will help your child on their way to making new friends as most, if not all, of them have been used in my sessions.

The Friendship Code

THE TOOL TO USE

Friendship tool

There is a tool called the Friendship Code and it can be very useful for your child to help define what they need in terms of a friend and a friendship. The code is made up of a list of what makes a 'good' friend and then it is turned into your child's own 'friendship code' so they can remind themselves of what is and is not acceptable from a friend.

1 Find a piece of paper or card and some felt-tips and sit with your child.

2 Write on the top of the paper or card 'A good friend for me is someone who ...'

3 Ask them, 'What do they look for in a friend?'

4 Make a list of everything they say under the heading. The list should contain attributes and traits such as 'polite', 'kind', 'keeps secrets', 'someone I can trust', 'shares', 'friendly', 'caring' and 'generous'.

5 They can decorate the paper or card and put it in their bedroom. It keeps hold of their values regarding friendships and holds on to how they want to be treated.

What does your child need from their friends? Is it loyalty, generosity, a deep thinker, a sense of humour?

Mean friends

If your child complains to you that they have a mean friend who they would like to stop being unkind to them, find out why they want to be around this person. There may be something that they really love about the person or they may feel they have a hold over them and they are worried about breaking friends with them. If your child feels unhappy because they are not treated well by another person there are things that you can do.

Ajay had a mean friend who would sometimes play with him and sometimes not. When he was with other boys from the class the mean friend would call him rude names. Ajay and I made a list of options describing ways that he could stop the name-calling. Our list looked like this:

- Ignore him.
- Play with someone else.

- Walk away.
- Say, 'Why did you say that?' Think, 'Is the name-calling true? No, it is not.'
- Say something funny back (e.g. If his friend tells him that he smells, respond back with 'That is nice', 'Oh yes, I have not had a shower for ages' or just 'I know.')

Ajay wanted to use all of them but finally went for playing with other children and thinking to himself, 'What you are saying is not true'. His mean friend got bored of saying things to him so it definitely worked.

Another example of friends behaving in a mean way is Mark's friend Charlie.

Charlie used to ruin the games Mark was playing with other friends at break time. Charlie would do things like take the ball off Mark and his friends when they were playing football and go over to another area of the playground with it. Mark would then have to try and reclaim the ball while everyone else stood around waiting.

Mark liked Charlie but also felt sorry for him. He was stuck for what to say to him without hurting his feelings; however, he knew he had to stop Charlie from being disruptive. Mark and I came up with a list of 'considerate' options:

- Mark could say, 'We would love you to join in our game but it is no fun if someone ruins it.'

- Request that Charlie plays but if he tries to sabotage the game again he will not be allowed to join in next time.
- Ignore him and his attempts to ruin it.
- Suggest with his other friends that they play something else.
- Tell him that he cannot join in this game but you will play with him another time.

Mark decided to say to Charlie that he would like him to play but not if he was going to disrupt the game. It worked for a few days, but then Charlie started being disruptive again so Mark suggested to his other friends that they play something else which Mark said, 'worked better'.

If your child has a mean friend try and find a way together of how they can stop the meanness. Explain to your child that they have a choice to change the situation and by not doing anything about the person or the situation they are accepting it.

Feeling left out

It is not a nice feeling being left out but unfortunately at some stage most children are. It could be that they were not picked for a team game or that their friends all get together at the weekend and they aren't asked. Either way it amounts to the same thing: they are left out and their feelings are hurt. Children will always mention being left out as part of a conversation about friendships during a session and when I tap them for more information I realise that the left out feeling is recent and is not about being left out over a long period of time.

When your child says they are always left out ask them, 'What happened the rest of the day or the week?' and 'What did they do and how did it make you feel?'

Get them to bring back the balanced thought that they are not always left out and get them to perhaps write down over a week the inclusions from friends. Notice I did not write 'exclusions'. I want your child to think positively and see the good stuff going on in their life.

Children may say they are being left out and feel that way because when their friends are standing around talking and they go to join them, their peers carry on the conversation. Does your child think they should stop their conversation and if their friends don't does it mean that they are being left out? It could mean quite the opposite. It could mean their friends are comfortable with them joining the conversation and happy for them to listen in. The alternative is that their friends change the subject and then your child really would feel left out. I know from experience that when I join a group of friends and say, 'What are you talking about?' and they say, 'Nothing'. Nothing means boring or not of much interest; it does not mean that my friends are talking about me.

If your child feels left out by a friend and it is very real for them and they want to talk about it, then they could approach the friend that they feel is leaving them out. Perhaps they could call them when they are not at school or go round and see them to find out what's going on. It is important for your child to be open with their feelings as it may be that their friend is not aware they are doing it. When is the best time for your child to call them or drop round? What would they say to them? Practise some role-play so they feel more comfortable about speaking up and get them to think of what they want to achieve by the end of the conversation. Do they want to be best friends with them again or do they want their friend's behaviour to change?

Want to be friends with everyone

All children like to be liked and included in everything. Is it really possible to get on with everyone?

> Hattie thought so. She tried to get everyone in her class to like her so that she could be popular. She used to give the other children her belongings to keep and let them share all her things, including her lunch. Hattie and I talked about why people like each other and become friends. I explained to her that true friendships are built on personality and that if you are kind to other people, can be trusted, are polite and respect others then other children will want to spend

time with you. I got her to write down what she thought she had to offer her friends in terms of attributes and she came up with a lovely long list. By doing this activity, she could see that she had lots to offer others without having to give them presents. She could just be herself. She understood that the people who would gravitate towards her and want to be her friend would be the people who want her for her personality. Hattie and I had a few weeks' break so she could see what would happen when she stopped giving away her things. She found that a few people still asked her for belongings. To those people she said she would share her things but wanted them back afterwards and they did. Nothing changed with her other friends. They said nothing and continued to be her friends.

In reality your child will not get on with everyone and will not always be invited to everyone's birthday parties. It is important to relay to them that no amount of people pleasing will get them liked by everyone. Some children will happily take the free gifts but still not want to be friends with them.

Toxic friends

There are some children who we know are not good for our children. For whatever reason, they do not have our child's best interests at heart and can possibly abuse their friendship. The toxic friend may not always be kind to your child or they may make jokes about them. If you heard the jokes they made you would know there were hidden truths behind them. However, because your child wants to be friends with them they don't see the undercurrent of the jokes. Taking the mickey out of other people is not nice but it makes the toxic friend feel much better about themselves while the jokes and the sarcasm can really damage your child's self-esteem. Toxic friends can also try and squash others' dreams and make them doubt their ability.

When dreams and goals are questioned by others it is not a good feeling. Friends are supposed to be supportive and encourage you to do well. If your child has a friend who is unsupportive and discouraging then you can help them protect themselves and ignore the hurtful things their friend says. You can do this by building up your child's self-esteem so that 'sticks and stones don't break their bones' and explain to your child that perhaps their friend is jealous of what they can achieve or of what they have. Encourage your child to continue to do well and believe in them so that they have the support from home.

Toxic friends can also try to monopolise your child and their time and stop them from seeing other friends. A toxic friend can make your child feel guilty being friends with others. It can be sign of insecurity and control. If this is the case with your child, help them assert themselves and perhaps suggest that they speak to their toxic friend.

They could explain to them how it makes them feel and that actually if they were 'allowed' to be friends with others you could all be friends together.

If your child wants to continue being friends with the toxic friend they can but they need to accept that that is who they are. It may be that their toxic friend brings positive aspects to their life. Perhaps you should find out what these are. When I speak to children who have a toxic friend they will always point out their good points and play down the 'toxicity' despite mentioning it in the first place. You could suggest to your child that perhaps they should close the door on the friendship. How would that make them feel and how do they think the friend would take it? If they were to go down this route would they actually say that they did not want to be friends any more or would they just detach themselves from them. The other option they may be interested in doing is for them to slow down the friendship by seeing less of each other or seeing them as part of a group.

These are decisions your child must make. What would they have to lose if they broke friends with them? Do they feel able to continue being friends but not such close ones? Remind them that losing an unhealthy friendship is not the end of the world, especially if your child is very sociable and has lots of friends. If your child is shy it may be that they feel safe with this toxic friend and don't want to break away. If they want your help and they are shy perhaps you could invite some other children round to your house so that they can get to know some other children. Later down the line they may have the confidence to break away.

Ben had a toxic friend who wasn't very kind to him, but he liked him because he was popular. The toxic friend, Patrick, was very bossy and Ben was beginning to get fed up with it. We had a chat about his 'friend' Patrick and what Ben could do about him so that he was less bossy. I explained to Ben that we cannot change someone else's actions but what we can do is change our own. If Ben was going to do something different to protect himself, what would it be?

- He could say something to Patrick and ask him to be less bossy.
- He could say nothing, ignore the bossiness and walk away.
- He could spend less time with him.

After weighing up the pros and cons of each option, Ben chose to spend less time with Patrick so that he was not so affected by the unkind things he said and was not bossed around. Over time Ben realised that he did not need to be friends with Patrick and that there were lots of other children he could play with.

As a parent if you are concerned about the way a friend of your child's is being treated then ask them:

- Are you happy with the friendship?
- What part are you unhappy about?
- What would you change about that person?
- What could you do differently to protect your feelings or to get less upset or angry?

Look together at all the options that your child could do – in their thoughts and actions.

Peer pressure

We have a lot of control over our children when they are young but as they get older they start listening to their peers and are influenced by their tastes, the possessions they have and their advice. They want to do the same things as their friends, act the same way and even speak like them. Children want to be doing the same as their friends because they want to fit in and feel like they belong to a peer group. However, your child may not want to be doing what their friends are. If they don't, you may need to help them resist the peer pressure.

There are plenty of children who want to say no to the pressure they feel from their friends because they know what their friends are doing is not right. As a coach working mainly with primary-school-aged children, I am talking about stealing, smoking, backchat, misbehaving in school, etc.

If your child wants to start saying no more often or thinking more for themselves without peer influence you can help them by:

- Talking about your family values. Children like to be a part of something so if you make your child feel like they are part of your family group, you will be able to build strong family values. Do your children know what these values are? By talking and reinforcing them your child will re-learn the behaviours and attitudes that are acceptable in your family and realise that not all families have the same values, hence why some of their friends are doing things that they aren't!

- Sharing your thoughts and feelings on what is going on inside and outside of the house. For example, what you think about smoking or stealing. They will hopefully value your thoughts and take on board what is important to you. Ask them what they think of some of the things you mentioned.

- Working on their self-esteem. You can build them up so they don't feel they need or have to be part of a group to fit in or feel good about themselves (see Chapter 6 on self-esteem). Building a healthy sense of self-esteem in your child means that they will be able to resist the pressure from others to do something against their wishes when they have said no.

- Giving them an open door policy whereby they can come to you with their problems so you can discuss them together and get them to think about how they could solve them. If they find it hard to come up with solutions then help them along a bit. Use the probing questions, 'What do you want to happen?', 'Why?' 'When?', 'How?'

When it comes to peer pressure what do you think your child would respond to more?

Shy children

Despite your child being shy it is still very important that they are able to build and maintain positive peer relationships in and out of school. Having a shy child should not mean loneliness and it should not be a barrier to making friends. What it does mean is that they may ask for a bit more help from you than an outgoing child when it comes to making friends. If they want some guidance from you, you can:

- Help them interact with small groups of children by suggesting to them that they invite some classmates to your house after school or at the weekend. The smaller group will mean they will have a chance to talk to each child and get to know them away from the hustle and bustle of school life.

- Introduce them to hobbies where they can make friends with children who enjoy the same activities, such as football, dance or drama lessons, Brownies, etc. Many parents feel that drama can really build confidence in a child and help shyness because the child has to get involved in singing, dancing, etc. and there is a lot of role-playing involved. Children will often find it easier to talk to someone when they are doing the same thing. For example, they have to talk to each other when playing football, otherwise how else will someone pass the ball to them? What activity would they like to do? Perhaps there is someone they already know doing that activity who they would like to go with. Going with a friend will make the new activity less daunting.

- Suggest to their teacher that they work in a team rather than working alone, but check with your child first to make sure that they are happy for you to speak to their teacher about group work. Your child may like working alone and perhaps even chooses to do so. If they are reticent about being part of a group explain the benefits to them. For example, sharing ideas and learning together will be more fun and your child will get to share the responsibility of the project rather than it just being theirs.

- Get them to think of the other people in their class. If they had to make one friend in their class who would it be? Who do they like and respect and who has shared interests?

Finally, talk about who they are and how much you love who they are. They may be shy but they are a wonderful human being.

Fighting versus compromise and negotiation

If only friendships were easy and there was never a cross word said between your child and their friends. Can you imagine that? It would make for a boring world because it would mean your child and their friends would all have the same opinion, be agreeable with whatever anyone else said and would all feel the same in the same situation. They would all be generic.

Children have arguments because they are different in their views, thoughts and feelings. Some children find it hard to accept others have these differences and will want to fight, shout or use aggression to get their point across.

Daniel, aged eight, wanted everything his way and did not like to compromise with his friends. It was his way or the highway. In our sessions we talked about how everyone has different ideas about things, different needs and wants and that to make other people happy, we have to consider their feelings and desires as well as our own. What was Daniel not prepared to compromise on? Well, he loved to play football and always wanted to be in goal. His friends always wanted to be in goal but he would not let them. They would get angry with him and refuse to play with him. I asked him how would he feel if he wasn't goalie but got to still play with his friends? He said he would be unhappy. How would he feel if one of his friends refused to let him be a goalie for any part of the game they were playing? He said he would be sad. What if he played in goal for 10 minutes and then let someone else be in goal? He said he would be happier. He was saying that he was prepared to share his goalie time.

I explained the importance of thinking of others and we discussed how he feels when someone is considerate to him. We used heaps of examples. He realised that actually he was being selfish and would be involved in fewer fights and shouting matches if he 'compromised'. The hardest part of implementing this would be him remembering what he needed to do and the results it would give him. By being less aggressive and slightly more agreeable, his friends would be happier playing football with him.

Daniel and I talked for ages about the benefits of compromising and the thought process he had to have and when he left my session he kept on going over and over in his head what he had to do. When I saw him next he proudly told me he had been getting on better with his friends *playing football and that he did not miss being in the goal all the time that much.*

If you have a child who generally finds fighting easier than talking, or negotiating, what can you do? Can you get them to think about what they are really fighting about? If it is a matter of opinion, can they just agree to disagree or walk away? Can they be less proud? Can they recognise that they are getting upset or angry in a situation and calm themselves down by using anger management techniques (see Chapter 4 on feelings). Can they negotiate with their friends by saying, 'You can have a go now, and then it will be my turn.' I don't believe fighting and shouting resolve anything. I think a good discussion can get the same results.

If your child finds it hard to negotiate you could try role-playing the difficult situation where they find it hard to back down on what they want. Then when they are on their own they can try it out. This will develop their problem-solving skills.

Speaking up

What about if you have a child that feels like they are being walked all over? They don't feel they have a voice and let others boss them around. How do they negotiate and get what they want or need? If your child feels strongly about something that is happening, they may need help with speaking up so they don't feel frustrated and annoyed with themselves. Why aren't they speaking up for themselves? What are they afraid of?

Ask your child what would happen if they spoke to their friend and said, 'I don't agree' or 'I don't want to...'. What do they think their friend would say or do? For example, if your child wants to play with their friends but does not want to play the game they are currently playing could they suggest the game they want to play? Their friends may welcome the idea of a different game, perhaps one they have not played for a while. Alternatively, if your child is unhappy with the rules because one person has made them up and they do not think they are fair encourage them to speak up. Other people changing or dominating the rules of a game can cause distress to your child because they know they are not the correct rules. They need to decide if they play the game or not.

How assertive is your child when it comes to negotiating and compromise? What kind of skills could you teach them so they could stand up for themselves more and say what they want or need from other people?

Being assertive

It can be hard to teach your child how to be assertive. I think role-playing is a great tool to use so your child practises speaking up – asserting their feelings and thoughts – or they can practise backing down slightly so they are not overpowering their friends and making them feel that they are being aggressive towards them.

ROLE-PLAYS

An example of role-playing being assertive:

You: 'Let's go and annoy Freddie.'

Child: 'No.'

You: 'Go on – it is always fun when we annoy him because he cries like a baby.'

Child: 'Actually, I don't want to any more as I don't think it is kind.'

You: 'It has never stopped you before – come on.'

Child: 'No, it is okay. I'm going to play bulldog with Jack.'

Another example is:

You: 'You're coming back to play at mine after school.'

Child: 'Yes, I know but I don't really want to as I don't like playing the games you do.'

You: 'Why not?'

Child: 'Well, they are boring so I don't want to come.'

You: 'But we arranged for you to come to my house and I would really like you to.'

Child: 'Okay, but can we only play that game for a little while and then do something I like?'

Personal space

Personal space is a tricky area that you need to teach your children and it is not a concept that is easy to grasp. I have seen children that literally stand on top of another child and talk to them or they touch the other child too much and you can see the other child squirming. Everyone needs space to move, breathe and talk.

It is important for children to learn about personal space as it can help them make and keep friends.

THE TOOL TO USE

Personal space tool

1 Ask your child to stand up in front of you so that your feet are touching.

2 Get them to take one step back and explain to them that this is the right amount of space there needs to be when they are speaking with their friends. This is a reasonable amount of space to talk. Any closer can be uncomfortable for the other person.

Explain to your child that touching with permission is a great way to connect with their friends and explain to them the type of touching that other children would be okay with. Touching can make other people feel special and loved. I would say it is okay to touch friends on the arm and hug them if they are good friends as and when. It is when the touching becomes more frequent and if it is on the face or legs that it can become a problem. Show them the kind of touch they can do to friends on the arm or the kind of hug that friends like to receive.

If it is your child who is being crowded and touched in a way they don't like by other people, talk to them about how they could communicate this to the touchee that is kind and considerate. One way is to say, 'I really like spending time with you but sometimes I feel crowded. Could you maybe stand a bit further away from me when you speak' or 'I really like spending time with you but I would prefer it if you did not touch me.'

Mind-reading

Mind-reader – 'A person who can supposedly discern what another person is thinking' – *Oxford Dictionary*.

Mind-reading seems to go on a lot in friendships. All it takes is for a child to see two of their friends chatting to each other and looking in their direction for them to assume that they are talking about them. Mind-reading or second guessing, as I call it, is assuming that you know what someone else is thinking. It is a dangerous game to play and it can change how your child feels about themselves.

> *Charlotte came to see me because she was having friendship problems. She thought that her friends were talking about her because they were whispering and looking over at her at the same time. I asked her what she thought they were saying. She said, 'Well I am not sure but it was clear they were talking about me.' I asked her to look for the evidence that they were indeed talking about her. Could she hear them? The only thing that was evident was that two of her friends were talking together. I explained they could have been planning a surprise for her, talking about someone or something else. They may have been looking at her and thinking how wonderful she was or how they liked her shoes or hair. She thought about the possibilities and realised that because she did not have any firm evidence that they were*

talking about her then she would have to accept that they could have been talking about anything. If she really needed to know what they were saying then she would have to ask them straight out. Charlotte did not think this was a good idea so she decided, after our discussion, that she would take no notice when her friends were talking without her. She would think to herself, 'They could be saying anything. I have no evidence it is about me.' Once she started thinking like this her friendship problem disappeared.

I don't think it is obvious to some children that their friends may be having an innocent conversation. Because they are being looked at they automatically think they are the main topic of conversation. If you find your child mind-reads boost their self-esteem a bit as well as challenging the reality. The mind-reading should go away as quickly as it came.

Regarding everything to do with your child's friendships, remember to keep the line of communication open between you and your child so that you can support them through the tough times with their friends. Don't interfere – just make your feelings clear about the situation and let them know that you are there for them.

Checklist

- Friendships are not easy.
- Children need to find like-minded peers.

- Good friendships take time to develop.
- Share your values to reduce peer pressure.
- Friendships require compromise and negotiation.
- Encourage your shy child to join in activities.
- Mind reading affects your child's self-esteem.

chapter six

How to help your child accept and like who they are

'Never bend your head. Hold it high. Look the world straight in the eye'
HELEN KELLER

What is self-esteem?

Self-esteem is how you feel and the beliefs you hold about yourself. It is about accepting your weaknesses as well as your strengths and being able to see the world as it really is. Self-esteem is also about accepting what you are capable of. It means never rating yourself – good, bad, useless, etc., only aspects of yourself – for example, 'I am not brilliant at cooking but that is fine because I am good at so many other things'. Children need to love who they are and accept that they are unique. They will be great at some things and not others. They can't be good at every-thing and should be encouraged to like themselves on the inside and the outside.

It is important that we raise children to have a healthy

self-esteem so that they are able to handle the tough times that they will have in life, as well as the good. Children who feel good about themselves seem to have an easier time handling conflicts and resisting negative pressures. They tend to smile more easily and they are more realistic and generally optimistic. Children with high self-esteem don't let what others say to them or about them affect the way they think about themselves. They are balanced in their thoughts.

Self-esteem can also be determined with feelings of being loved. Children who are generally happy with what they achieve but don't feel loved may experience low self-esteem. And children who feel loved but do not feel confident in their ability can also end up with low self-esteem.

If your child has a healthy self-esteem they will be able to:

- Act independently.
- Assume responsibility.
- Take pride in their abilities.
- Deal with their emotions.
- Willingly accept new challenges.
- Handle problems efficiently.

Children with low self-esteem are completely different. They can get anxious and frustrated when faced with a new challenge and can have a hard time finding solutions to problems as they immediately think, 'I can't do this'.

Your child with low self-esteem may:

- Feel unloved and unwanted.
- Blame others for their own mistakes.
- Avoid taking on new challenges or tasks.
- Put themselves down.
- Discredit their own abilities.
- Be easily influenced or manipulated by others.

The importance of self-esteem

Wouldn't it be great if with a swish of a wand we could make all children feel confident and sure of themselves? After all that is what most parents want for their children. We want them to have a healthy self-esteem. Unfortunately, not all children do as when they enter new situations and experiences they are exposed to other people's thoughts and feelings. They can have a tendency to compare themselves to other people and when they don't do well in something they may feel disheartened to try again.

I see a lot of children as young as six years old who have low self-esteem. Low self-esteem can begin in a thousand different ways. It could be a throwaway comment that someone has said to them or it may be they have not received the recognition of doing a job well that they think they deserved. That comment or lack of comment can make them feel down and make them believe they are not a good person or that they are not good at something. Some children are unable to put the comment or situation into context and see the bigger picture and so their self-esteem suffers. When we recognise that our child has low self-esteem we can often try and analyse where it has come from, but it is more important that we look forward, using the coaching process, and tackle it. What we need to do is get rid of the horrible thoughts that your child has about themselves and make them feel on top of the world once again. There is a whole section in Chapter 10 on how to get rid of negative thoughts and achieve more balanced ones. In this chapter I want to show you how you can help your child accept who they are.

What kind of self-esteem has your child got? How do you recognise it?

An example of how easily healthy self-esteem can be affected:

> *In my early days of being a coach I worked with six-year-old Rachel who believed that she was not very clever because her friends were reading and writing and she wasn't. She said she wanted to be as good as her friends in her school work. I asked her if she thought that everyone was able to do the same things as everyone else at the same time. She was not sure so I asked her if her friends could ride a bike. She said no but she could. Ah, then if she could ride a bike and her friends couldn't and her friends could read but they could not ride a bike then everyone must be different. So what else could she do? What was she good at? We made a long list and she was able to understand that she could do lots of things. We talked about how everyone learns at different paces and that she is still learning and she does not have to be good at all of her school work. She can only try her best and the skills needed for reading and writing would come in their own time. The coaching sessions were a success!*

If your child feels a similar way to Rachel, you can ask them:

- What are you good at? (Make a list.)
- What do you think you should be good at? (Make another list.)

- Why do you think you should be good at that list? What evidence shows that you should be good at it?
- Is everyone good at everything they turn their hand to?

Share with them what your strengths are and what you are not so good at, and also explain to them that we all learn at different stages because our brain takes time to develop and retain information.

I also worked with a boy of 10 called Alex, who did not have very many friends because he saw himself as not having very much to offer others. He felt he was an under-achiever, did not do anything exciting and therefore did not have a lot to contribute to a conversation with his peers. We worked on the area of building friendships in a later session, but first we talked about his self-esteem. I established he did not feel his self-worth because the people around him were doing well at school and he was comparing himself to them. He wanted to be more like his friends – confident, easy-going and comfortable with themselves, something he was not. I tried to get him to talk about the attributes he had but he found it difficult so we started to get creative using some of the ideas I mention in this chapter. In doing so he started to see that actually he had lots to offer and potentially had lots to talk about, too.

There are so many ways to help your child to build up their self-esteem and the process can be one that takes weeks, months or even years. We need to invest that time in our children so they are happier and emotionally stronger within themselves and with the world around them so they can cope with life.

Ideas to start feeling great

The square

Draw a square and make it into four equal smaller squares by drawing a line down the centre both horizontally and vertically. In each smaller square list the headings 'Things I am good at', 'Things people say about me' (good stuff only), 'My achievements' and 'My qualities' and in the middle write the word 'ME' in big letters. Under each heading ask your child to write things about themselves so they can see clearly who they are, what they have achieved and what they are good at.

I love this activity and find that when dealing with self-esteem, practical exercises really work. The square can also be done using a flower, apples on a tree or a train with carriages depending on the age of the child.

Wheel of strength

A variation of the square idea is the wheel of strength. This is where your child fills in parts of the wheel with a list of strengths (qualities, skills, talents, abilities) that they have. They then choose their top three and write a statement underneath the wheel that provides evidence that they have these strengths. For example, 'I am patient because my teacher tells me', 'I am creative because I come up with lots of ideas'. You can do this with your child and also have a wheel for yourself so you both share the experience. Doing an activity together like this can be a great time to talk and swap ideas.

You could even go a step further and decide on something they want to achieve in the near future. How could they use one of their strengths to reach this achievement?

The A to Z

Another great creative way to tackle low self-esteem is to use the alphabet. Get a large piece of paper and write the alphabet, A to Z, down the left-hand side. Then on the right-hand side ask your child to think of a word for each letter that best describes them and jot it down. Some of the words are quite easy but when you get to the likes of X, Y and Z, it gets trickier! You may have to help them here.

Self-esteem diary

I am a big fan of diaries for all different types of reasons but in the case of self-esteem it is one activity I think that can really help. Buy or find your child a diary or an exercise book and get them to decorate it if they fancy it. By decorating it, it will feel more personal to them. Next, get them to start using it. Everyday just before they go to bed get them in the routine of writing a self-esteem journal where they can list new qualities they have discovered about themselves and record compliments that they have received from other people. They could even rate how good the compliments made them feel out of 10.

The self-esteem diary could also be a place for your child to record their achievements and put in positive quotes that they find. All of these things will help make them see themselves and their life in a new and positive light. Your child may want to just have a diary where they only record compliments and that is okay.

Go with how they want to use it. Whichever way that is, it will still raise their self-esteem and make them feel good about themselves.

Diaries don't just have to be used to boost self-esteem. They can also be useful for stresses and thoughts. If your child is anxious and cannot sleep why not suggest to them that they empty their thoughts on paper before going to bed. Your child could also diarise events that have not gone as smoothly as they hoped so they can reflect back and think of other ways they could have handled them. These new ideas can be written down in their diary and referred to in the future.

Collage of identity

Find a piece of A3 paper and a pile of old magazines and get your child to cut out pictures from the magazines that they feel reflect them and their personality. They may cut out their favourite food, an image of the sport they like doing, games, words, cartoons, etc. By doing a collage of their feelings and interests, they will be able to see clearly who they are and perhaps think about what they want to achieve in life. The collage is a great way to build up a sense of identity – a key element of self-esteem.

A silhouette of me

Children love this activity as it is so much fun. Ask your child to lie down on the floor on a huge piece of paper, draw around them and cut it out. Together, within the silhouette, write their name, age, height, favourite things, interests, likes, things they are good at, etc. The silhouette will help remind them and appreciate who they are.

Certificates

My final way to boost self-esteem is to use certificates or achievements. If your child does not have any certificates perhaps you could make your own certificates and give them to your child when they do something well. For example, they could get a certificate for laying the table well for a week or for being generous and kind.

Which self-esteem boosters do you think would be well received by your child?

All these self-esteem activities work but they are of no real benefit to a child unless they are placed somewhere where they will see them regularly (but the diary – that should be hidden away). Ask your child where they think they should put the artwork or collage so that it is somewhere prominent and they will be able to see it every day. Perhaps they could place it on their bedroom wall or inside a cupboard so they see it every time they get their clothes out. It will remind them of what makes them special, what they can offer others and the reasons why they should feel good about themselves. I think it is always lovely to walk into a child's room and see certificates up on the walls and pictures and photos of special people in their lives. Achievements can have their own celebratory board.

> *Julian decided to make a monthly 'WOW' board. On it he would list his achievements. He used a whiteboard and laid it out as the table opposite.*

WOW BOARD							
	Monday	Tuesday	Wednesday	Thursday	Friday	Saturday	Sunday
Week 1					Got star pupil		
Week 2			3 house points				
Week 3	Invited to party						
Week 4				Completed reading book			

Everyday before he went to bed he wrote down all his home and school achievements on it. Because the 'WOW' board only covered a month, at the end of each month, he would write down his achievements in an exercise book that he could put in a drawer in his bedroom to remind himself of what he had achieved. The 'WOW' board was wiped clean and used for the following month. I saw Julian after a few weeks of using the board and he said he found it really useful and reminded him of any achievement, big or small, that he would normally forget.

The activities I have talked about all encourage thinking and creativity and can be done by your child alone or with you. You can also help your child with their self-esteem by using positive verbal cues like praise and compliments.

The importance of praise

THE TOOL TO USE

Self-esteem tool

1 Use praise whenever your child has done something well or has shown that they have tried.

2 No matter how big or small the task is, be as descriptive as you can in your praise.

3 Use sentences like, 'Thank you for putting the dishes in the sink, you are a really helpful child,' or 'You were great at taking turns on the computer today with your friend – what a wonderful sharer you are.' Descriptive praise tells your child specifically what they have done well and it makes them feel great about themselves.

4 Alongside praise give your child a high five or a huge hug. Make any excuse to celebrate their successes.

5 If you want to praise your child, but want to use a way that feels natural to you as a parent, perhaps you could write them a note outlining how great they are and how proud you are of them.

By telling our children that we believe in them, we are letting them know that they are great individuals and that we love them.

Compliments are also another wonderful way to make children feel good and confident about what they are doing.

Try and make your children feel special by noticing the little things that they do well. A great indirect way of complimenting your child is by talking about them in front of them. For example, when they are standing near you and you know they can hear, you could say to your friend, 'Did I tell you how well Katie did in . . . I am so proud of her.'

Self-esteem is not all about your child feeling great – it is also about celebrating their uniqueness.

Celebrating uniqueness

'*Always be a first-rate version of yourself, instead of a second-rate version of somebody else*' JUDY GARLAND

No two children are the same and while we love the uniqueness of our child being absorbed in 'science', for instance, your child may worry that they are not the same as other children and aren't fitting in with their peers. They don't want to be unpopular and they don't want to stop doing what they love. How can they fit in, carry on being who they are and keep their passion for the 'stuff' that makes them who they are? As parents we can really help them. We can:

- Get them to celebrate their unique qualities and make reference to the attributes that they have and keep to what they believe in. For example, they may not be very tall but they may be good at running and dodging people while playing football.

- Make them realise that getting noticed for being different is good, if not now but later on in life. Who wants to be the same as other people? There is nothing wrong with being a little quirky. To be able to bring something different to the conversation makes life more interesting. For instance, your child may know lots about science when their friends don't, but their friends may be interested in hearing all about the experiments your child does at home.

- Explain to them that getting noticed brings with it interest from others. Explain to your child that people will be interested in what they are saying, just not everyone all the time. They need to find the right group of friends for them so they feel appreciated for who they are. That can take time but as I say it is better to find the right friends and for it take longer than for them to make the wrong friends because they are desperate to make friends.

- Lead by example. If we are comfortable in our own skin our children will see that and hopefully let go of any hang-ups and insecurities that they have about themselves. The same goes for if we stand up for what we believe is right. Your children will be more likely to speak their mind if they see you do it.

How do you help your children be who they are?

We can also help them celebrate their uniqueness by allowing them to 'get to know and understand' themselves. We can help them do this by:

- Giving them some quiet time. Quiet time will give them the space to stop thinking about everything that is going on around them and just listen to their own thoughts and feelings.
- Coaching and guiding them. Ask them about their feelings and thoughts about things, help them to solve their problems if they ask for your help and guide them through situations they are having difficulty with.
- Helping them to be reflective. When they do something positive or negative help them to reflect on what they did so that they can see the consequences of their actions. For example, asking them, 'What went well when you did that?' or 'What did you learn?'
- Encouraging them to think about what they are doing. If you always tell your child what to do they will learn to do as they are told without questioning what you say. If you

teach them to reason and think for themselves you will find that they will be able to think and plan ahead on their own, hence making them more responsible for their actions. The same goes for problem solving. If you always solve your child's problems they will not be able to do this for themselves when they are older and will run back to you for every decision they need to make. As parents, this is probably not what we want to happen. We want our children to be independent and be able to make informed decisions.

Which of the above do you think you could do more of?

If we help equip our children with good self-esteem, if and when they encounter problems from their peers they will have the ability to emotionally deal with them.

Verbal cues to help with self-esteem

Children need to recognise that they are capable of doing things for themselves and can do them well. We can help them do this by getting them to see what they are already competent in. For example, they may say that they cannot do something but, with some encouragement, they will see that they can load the dishwasher, pack their bag for school or water the plants. They just think they can't because they have either never done it before or they have not done it for a while. If your child needs help with a new experience offer it, and if they take you up on it, teach them the right way. By asking our children to do more for themselves and take more responsibility for their belongings, we are indirectly saying to them, 'We trust you and know you will do a good job.' This will, in turn, help their self-esteem.

We can also give our children the self-esteem they need by:

- Praising them when they have done something well or when they have done something without asking. Descriptive praise can really boost their self-esteem especially when it is totally unexpected.
- Encouraging them to be independent. We can do this by getting them to take chances and try new things. Succeeding in something new can give children a huge boost to their self-esteem.
- Asking our children for their opinion on things that we are doing and getting them involved in making decisions that will affect them. Your child will feel valued that they have been asked and listened to.
- Teaching our children to make good decisions. You

could get them involved in some of the smaller decisions you make as a way of learning to make good choices. Once your child learns to exercise sound judgement they have shown responsibility, which in turn will raise their self-esteem.

- Reassuring them that when they struggle with a situation or task that it's okay to find it difficult and that sometimes we have to practise something a lot before we get it right. It does not mean they have failed or they are a failure. Tell them that you still don't get everything right, that we all make mistakes and that it's all part of growing up and learning. If we knew how to do everything where would the challenge be? Use kind and supportive words such as, 'I understand how you feel but I believe you can do it.' Encourage them all the way and, when they do get through the situation, celebrate their achievement.

- Listening and respecting our child's interests even if they don't interest us. If your child wants to talk to you about something – anything – make sure you have the time to listen and be enthusiastic, even if you don't feel the same passion as they feel for a subject. It will make your child feel that they are the centre of your universe.

- Avoiding saying negative things that may be hurtful to our children. Your child will always remember something said to them that was unkind.

I love all the ideas above but which of the above methods do you think would be well received by your child?

Beliefs

I want to finish this chapter with a section on beliefs because I feel it fits in best here. Some children really believe that if they do something they will get the desired outcome. For example, if they are generous and helpful then other people will like them or they may believe that if they work hard they will get good grades. Children need to get rid of these beliefs as they are assumptions and there are no guarantees in life. We can help them to have realistic beliefs and expectations by talking to them about all the outcomes of a situation. It is important to relay to your child that they should work hard to attain the grades they desire and if they don't then it won't be for lack of trying and putting the hard work in. We can help them by using words of encouragement that are going to motivate them to do and be their best.

Negative and fixed beliefs can be challenged by looking at the reality of the situation. I will talk more about this in Chapter 10, alongside the other life skills children want help with.

Checklist

- Self-esteem can affect your child's outlook on life.
- Visual aids can help your child's self-esteem.
- Help celebrate your child's uniqueness.
- Encourage your child to think for themselves and make good decisions.
- Give children age related responsibilities.
- Praise and compliment your child.

chapter seven

How to help your child get on better with their siblings

'If we have no peace, it is because we have forgotten that we belong to each other'   MOTHER TERESA

Sibling rivalry

For those of you who are not used to the term 'sibling rivalry', it is when siblings compete or are jealous of each other for some reason. The jealousy often manifests itself in squabbles, bickering and possibly physical fighting. There are lots of factors that can influence how often your children fight and how bad the fighting gets and it is based around how they feel. When a child's needs change, they feel anxious or unsure of themselves and are more likely to pick a fight with their sibling. For example, a new baby in the family can make a child feel pushed out or it can be as simple as one child playing with their new game and their sibling wanting to play with it as well.

Children often complain to me about their siblings being treated differently to them. It could be because their older sibling gets to stay up late or that their younger sibling gets more affection. Children believe in fairness (we know that because they will often say, 'But it is not fair') and equality ('But I had to have a bath') and don't like the fact that a brother or sister will be getting preferential treatment. I also know that slightly older children who have their own social life and like their independence can often resent having to look after a younger sibling. This situation has cropped up in my coaching sessions. It is not easy when you are 13 years old and chatting with your friends on Facebook to also have to look after your seven-year-old brother who wants to play a game with you. It is likely that you will get annoyed with their demands and questioning to get your attention. You would eventually have to stop using the computer and may start squabbling to reclaim your own space.

I think personality plays a huge role in how siblings get along. Often you find one child is very laid-back and the other is highly strung and energetic. The laid-back one often gives in to the other and the energetic one finds a way to annoy the laid-back one. I don't think sibling rivalry can be avoided 100 per cent.

Sibling rivalry is caused by:

- One child feeling they are getting less love and attention from a parent than their siblings.

- Possessiveness of toys, etc.
- A lack of fairness – time on the computer, for example, or favouritism – one always gets what they want and the other feels they are losing out.
- Comparisons being made between children.

Why do your children argue?

It is not easy getting on with everyone in your family, especially with brothers and sisters who are vying for the same attention as the child you are concerned about. Some siblings just get on with it. There are the few odd niggles but generally they respect each other, are helpful and considerate. But what do you do when your children aren't? In my clinic I see many children who want to talk about their relationships with their siblings. They find it really frustrating when their siblings annoy them and find themselves becoming angry and start physically or verbally fighting. The person who gets in a rage does not want to argue but they feel they have to defend their corner. One of the siblings always gets hurt (usually the youngest or the smallest), a parent comes in and someone gets told off and possibly punished. What needs to happen is for the child sitting in front of me, complaining about their siblings being mean to them, to make changes to how they are reacting to the situation so that either the arguments subside or the anger does not present itself.

By using the four types of sibling rivalry mentioned on the previous page, how can you help your children to get on better with their siblings?

Getting less love and attention from a parent than their siblings

How does your child feel when they perceive their siblings are getting more love? Why do they feel that way? What would they like to change so that they felt it was more equal?

> I saw a boy called Bailey who felt that his mum was spending more time saying goodnight to his brother than to him. Because Bailey wanted more of his mum's attention at bedtime he used to jeopardise his brother's night time routine by interrupting his story. To see if his mum was really saying goodnight for longer we did a challenge with his mum. We timed how long it took for her to say goodnight to both boys. The results showed it took her less time to say goodnight to Bailey than it did to his younger brother. Now we knew the reality of the situation, we could address the problem so that both children got the same about of attention at bedtime. Bailey needed to do this challenge for his own peace of mind and once he saw that actually he was getting less time from Mum, he was more than happy to get more.
>
> A similar thing happened with Jake. Jake's sister loved going shopping with her mum so when the two of them went

out, Jake stayed at home. Jake was jealous of his sister. He did not want to go shopping but he wanted to have the attention of his mum. When Jake's sister came home from shopping he would fight for his mum's attention and push his sister out of the way. How could I help Jake get what he wanted?

I asked him what he wanted. He wanted time with Mum. How much time did he want? He wanted a couple of hours. When? At the weekend. How did he want to spend his time with her? He would like to go bowling, to the cinema or to the park. When could he convey this to her? He could tell her after our session.

Jake told his mum and she did not realise that this was what he wanted. She said she would look in her diary and find a free weekend so that they could 'hang out' together.

It is very difficult to split your time fairly among however many children you have. If you can, make each one feel special by spending time each day talking and listening to them.

And what can you do when your child says they feel they are not getting the same amount of love from you as you give their siblings? Well, you can talk to them about why they feel that way. What would they like you to do about it? Do they want you to spend more one-to-one time with them or do they want more cuddles or rough and tumble? I know when my oldest feels left out of cuddles because he jumps on me while I am cuddling his brother. His actions speak volumes. He is saying, 'You are mine too.'

Having a new baby in the family may also contribute to sibling rivalry. As the dynamics change in the family with each child born, children can have an issue with having to share their parents. Babies take up time and timescales; jobs and plans can go out of the window. If your child is particularly keen to get things done and move fast then they may have difficulty with the pace a new baby brings. Children can also feel they are not getting as much time with their parents as they would like. If your child is telling you or displaying behaviour that shows that they are jealous or resent their new sibling then talk to them about their feelings and ask them, 'Why do you think that I have less time to spend with you and talk about the demands that a baby has.' What do they think you have to do when you have both them and the baby, and their other siblings? How are you going to do it all?

Explain to them that you will have less time but you will always have time for them. Get them to understand why they cannot do some of the things you used to do together. Explain that some things are not practical 'at the moment'. Talk about when you are going to spend time together. Put on a calendar when they will spend time with you so that they can see that they have something to look forward to. If it is every day then that is a great result for them. It is amazing how much 10 minutes of uninterrupted one-to-one time can mean to your child (and help their behaviour!).

There is always one part of the day that I think could be maximised and possibly monopolised by your child and that is when you are feeding the baby. It is a great opportunity for you both to have a chat and you can't escape! If you do get to spend an hour or so with your child let them choose the activity and follow their lead.

Possessiveness of toys, television progammes, electronic devices, etc.

It does not matter what toy, game or activity one of your children is playing with or doing, as soon as one of their siblings comes into the room they want to use it.

> Scarlett use to get really annoyed when her sister would come into the TV room and take over. Her sister would either change the channel on the TV or sit next to Scarlett at the computer and put her off the game she was playing. Scarlett came to see me because she wanted to handle both situations better. She was frustrated and at present was just letting her sister do what she wanted because she thought she would get into trouble for starting a fight with her sister if she stood up for her rights. We looked at the options of how Scarlett could handle the situation in an assertive manner rather than the passive way she had been displaying. She could:

- *Do nothing – not an option.*

- *Tell Mum or Dad – what would they do?*

- *Come up with a rule that there are no spectators when you are on the computer and you agree that when you have finished the other person can jump on it – would her sister buy into this idea?*

- *Suggest if one person is watching TV then the other has to wait for the programme to finish. In the meantime they can either watch it without interruption or go and do something else.*

Scarlett decided that out of all the options she wanted to draw up a mini contract that said that both she and her sister had to respect what the other person was doing and would have to wait to get what they wanted (i.e. their TV programme or time on the computer). Scarlett talked to her sister and she said she would give it a go at making it work. It took time and patience from both parties but they referred to the contract and after a couple of weeks they were getting on much better.

Ellie was another child that I saw who wanted to stop the fighting between herself and one of her siblings. She used to get upset when her younger sister snatched toys from her. Her options of what she could do about it were slightly different to those of Scarlett because her sister was only four years old. She could:

- *Tell her sister that she had the toy first and snatch it back – not a very good option, Ellie thought – 2/10.*

- *Suggest that they take turns – it could work – 7/10.*

- *Ellie could take something else to play with – she did not really want to do that – 4/10.*

- *Take another toy and give it to her younger sister and say how much better it was – she liked this idea, especially if she gave her sister her favourite toy – 8/10.*

- *Tell Mum and Dad – she did not think they would sort it out – 5/10.*

- Ignore her sister and just get on with doing something else – Ellie thought she would not be able to – 3/10.

Ellie decided after looking at all the options available to her that she would find another toy for her younger sister to play with or suggest taking it in turns. There were lots of other toys her sister loved to play with so Ellie could fetch her a couple. If they were going to take turns with the existing toy, then they would need to use the timer system. Her younger sister could have the toy for 10 minutes and Ellie could have it for 10 minutes after that. Ellie tried out both ideas to see which one her sister was more receptive to. As it happens, she liked both – it depended on the mood she was in at that time.

To recap, the timer system works by either you or the child setting a timer or stopwatch for a specific time so that they can either watch TV, use the laptop, play on the Playstation, etc. When the buzzer goes off the child knows that their time is up and it is the other person's go. This technique works well in many situations.

Lack of fairness or favouritism

This can be described as either giving one of your children something different to the other children you have or one child getting to do something that the other ones does not get to do. For example, you take one of your children to the park for ice cream while the other child goes to a birthday party. The child who did not get to go to the party may complain that they did not go to the party or the child who went to the party may complain they did not get to go the park.

Children like the fact that you treat them both the same and there is no favouritism. It does not even come into our minds that they have been treated unfairly. In the example of the party and the park both children would have had a good time doing something different and neither would have missed out. Children like fairness and like you to parent them the same way even though they are different. But each child has different emotional needs and therefore has to be parented differently. Some rules may be relevant to one child but not to the other.

For the child who has tougher rules and boundaries it will feel like they have got the rougher deal and they may feel like you are showing favouritism to your other children. For example, you have two children – one aged nine and the other aged five – who both have different chores to do at home. The nine-year-old has to load the dishwasher and the five-year-old has to set the table for mealtimes. The nine-year-old constantly moans about how unfair it is that they have to touch dirty dishes. Apparently you are favouring the other because 'all they have to do is to lay the table'.

I see many children who are unhappy about the division of labour. If your child complains about 'jobs' explain to them why you have chosen those jobs for them and explain to them that everyone has something to do so that the house runs well. What job would they prefer to do? Give them a list of jobs so they can pick one – hoover, clean their bedroom, wash the floors, make dinner, iron, etc. They will probably decide the one job they are doing is actually the best one. Do not let them decide on what their other siblings have to do!

Comparisons being made between children

It is easy to make comparisons between our children and we can do so unintentionally because they have different strengths, weakness and personalities. We notice that one of them is perhaps better behaved or better at something than their siblings and even if we don't say, 'You are much cleverer than your sister,' we may say, 'Why can't you be more like your brother or sister.' Children do not respond well to comparisons being made as it can lower their self-esteem as well as cause sibling rivalry. A better way to say something where you want one child to behave as the other one is to say something like, 'I would really like you to sit on your bottom like Freddy when at the dinner table,' rather than 'Why can't you sit like Freddy!'

Of course, siblings want to be as good as their brothers and sisters – the younger ones especially as they look up to their older siblings and want to be just like them. Regardless of age, it can still hurt a child when they don't feel as valued as their siblings.

It is important that we don't make comparisons between our children as we love them all the same. If your child feels less loved remind yourself to not compare them to their brothers and sisters and remind your child, and yourself, of their uniqueness. If comparisons are made your child may feel they cannot compete with the amazing behaviour of their sibling and therefore behave adversely to get your attention.

Sibling rivalry can be noisy and children do not enjoy fighting mainly because they know the consequences of what we are going to do if they don't work it out themselves or someone gets hurt. If we can give them the tools to stop, think and understand why they are upset then that is the first step forward.

What do your children fight over mainly? Is there one particular area that you could help them work on?

Finding a solution to sibling rivalry

Children are always going to be jealous of something their sibling has or they feel that somehow there has been an injustice made. As parents we can help our children deal with the rivalry between them and help to keep it manageable. We can do this by showing our children how to get along. We are role models for our children and everything we do they see and learn from. If we resolve problems at home in a way that is respectful, civilised and calm then our children are more likely to do the same. If we resolve problems by hitting, lashing out and screaming then they will do the same. What we need to do is show our children that when we want something someone else has we have to ask and when we want to be treated fairly we have to ask to have the same as someone else.

I think the one thing children want from their parents when it comes to sibling rivalry is to be saved. They want Mum or Dad to intervene and to stop the fighting. It is normally the person who is getting hurt who wants them to intervene so that Mum or Dad can comfort them and they will be given the thing they were fighting over. Splitting up your children when they are fighting is the easiest thing to do but it will not teach them how to resolve conflict.

Children need to fight their own battles rather than have someone else fight them for them. It is good for their self-esteem and there are going to be times in their lives when they will not have Mum or Dad around to intervene. For instance, if they were in the playground and one of their friends did not share or was getting more attention from another friend, would they tell the teacher? The answer is probably no because they would look silly.

So when your child comes to you for help about reducing their sibling squabbles, how can you help them?

- You can start by talking to them about how angry they feel about the situation they find themselves in with their sibling. Do they think they could be less angry? If they were they would find it easier to solve the problem or disagreement.

- You can ask them how important is it for them to have the same thing as their sibling? Or are they just picking a fight for no reason? What else could they do to get what they wanted without conflict? How else can your child get their sibling to share and be fair?

- You can ask them to be more conscious of what they are saying and how they are saying something to their brother or sister. Can they think, 'What would be the best way to say it?' and 'How is the other person going to respond?' It is not easy and requires practice.

Billy, aged seven, came to see me because his mum felt that he was always being nasty to his brother Tod. He would never ask him nicely for anything. For example, if Tod was looking at a magazine that belonged to Billy and Billy was doing something else he would still snatch it off him and say, 'That's mine, you can't have it, give it back to me'. Tod would say that he was just looking at it and that if Billy wanted it then he should ask for it. Billy refused to ask so an argument would start. Billy would then escalate the things he would say to his brother and Tod would get upset. Mum wanted the 'picking a fight for no reason' to stop and felt that Billy needed to learn that if he wanted something he had to ask for it.

Billy and I talked about the importance of asking for things and about how good sharing can be. I got him to role-play with me the type of words he could use to obtain his belongings so he could learn what the best thing to say would be. Billy decided he would ask in a calm way, use the word 'please' and say something like, 'I will let you read it but when you have finished please give it back to me'. He thought his brother would respond well to that and despite finding it difficult to let go of things that were his he was willing to try out the new approach. The next time his brother had something he wanted he would ask. Several weeks later we had another session and Billy said that his new approach was working.

- You could also teach your child to negotiate. An example of negotiation can be used when your children all want to be doing the same thing, like having a go on the computer. By all negotiating how much time they are all going to have, each makes it fair especially if they use my faithful tool of a stopwatch and time each other. The beep makes both of them and you aware that it is time to change players and you can't fool a stopwatch!

- You can help them by getting them to think of alternative ways of not fighting. Ways that use consideration, compassion and patience. Ask them when would they like to try out their new ideas? Why not straightaway? Talk to your child about when they would like you to intervene. Is it when they get hurt or when they start to feel scared in the situation?

THE TOOL TO USE

Sibling rivalry tool

1 When your children are arguing and they want you to intervene go in to them.

2 Say calmly, 'So what's happening here?'

3 Separate them if they are joined and get them to calm down.

4 Explain that you are not going to take sides but would like to know what is going on. You may need to keep them separated for a while – perhaps have them in different rooms until they are both calm and able to talk about what happened.

5 When your children are calm ask each child what started the argument and ask them what each child wanted to happen. Why didn't it happen? What can they do now to resolve the problem? What would be a fair thing to do?

6 Listen to your children's suggestions and list them sitting together.

7 Ask both of your children to choose the suggestion they think is the best. They may choose different suggestions. If so, go with both ideas.

8 Get them to role-play or talk about what they are going to do and what they should have done instead of argue. Get them to speak to each other with respect.

Knowing my children, they would probably laugh by the time they got to the role-playing bit or one of them would have backed down.

The above ideas help when the problem is sharing, but what if the problem is about attention and being treated differently?

One of the ways you can get your children to understand why they are treated differently is to get them to stand opposite each other and look at each other – without laughing. Ask each child to make an observation about the other such as 'they are taller than me' or 'they are funnier' or 'they like tidying up' and get them to recognise that they do not look the same, are not the same age and that they are capable of doing different things. You can also include in here the difference in needs and likes. One has more homework than the other, one likes to play football or play the piano, one is able to get dressed by themselves, has more pocket money because they buy their own clothes or gets to use Facebook because they are over 13. Make it clear to them that what their older brother or sister has now they will have when they reach that age. It might be an idea that you make a note of when the oldest child has been allowed to have a mobile phone or go with their friends on their own during the day so that you can remember.

Having their own space

Another issue that can cause sibling rivalry is space. If your child feels crowded and wants to be able to stay up late, read in their room without interference or watch a TV programme that is just for them, it is important to find a way of making it happen.

James used to squabble over games all the time with his sibling. His younger brother used to see him playing with a certain group of toys and destroy his game because he wanted James to play with him. James just wanted some space and time on his own playing with his toys without having to feel he had to let his brother play. How could he resolve this? Well, we looked at the times when his brother was not around and talked about if these were good times for him to play alone. He said that he did not think so. Another option we came up with was that he could find something else for his brother to play or he could make suggestions to him of things he could do in his room. It turned out that his brother liked to be close to him and got lonely playing on his own. James did not want his brother to feel unhappy so they made a pact. His younger brother could play in James's room but had to bring his own toys in. His younger brother was happy that he got to play near James and would not be alone.

To resolve most sibling rivalry squabbles, sharing, compromising and negotiation have to be used. Respecting other people's wishes and space is not easy but it is easily taught. If your child has difficulty understanding that they cannot have access to all their sibling's toys get them to imagine what it would feel like if their sibling came into their room and started playing with their toys, or if they helped themselves to the sweets they were eating without asking. Annoying, isn't it? If they can truly put themselves in other people's shoes they may be more thoughtful or considerate towards their sibling. The same goes for privacy; there needs to be a rule that if one of your children wants to go into another's room then they need to ask.

Finally, what we can do as parents is to make sure that our children know the rules for acceptable behaviour. Do they know there is to be no name-calling, shouting, hitting, throwing, etc.? The sibling rivalry won't go away but it can improve.

RULES

Write out the rules and put them somewhere prominent – fridge or cupboard door – for everyone to see. Ask your children to add some rules and discuss with them what they think the consequences should be. You could even have family meetings to discuss sibling issues once in a while where you can think of new ways of helping your children get along better.

Can you think of some family rules now that you would like to enforce?

Step-siblings and sibling rivalry

What can be made harder in a family environment is when two families come together from two broken-down marriages or bereavement and the children are forced to either live together on a permanent basis or on a part-time basis. Some children may find it really difficult to adjust to the needs and wants of the other children, and they also have to adjust to the way the other children have been brought up. There can often be different rules for the step-siblings than for them and their blood sisters and brothers.

I saw a family years ago who had come together from two marriages and they had a child each. I saw both of the children separately and they wanted to change the way the other child was treated. The rules and boundaries were very different for each child – one child was allowed to stay up late and the other had to go to bed early. The two children constantly argued with each other about bedtimes, about how much time they were spending with their natural parent and the fact that one of them felt their privacy was being invaded by the other. We talked about what each child wanted and then came up with a plan.

Child one wanted the rules to be the same for both children so I asked child one to come up with a few rules that they thought were necessary. I then got child two to come up with some rules, too.

The rules child one suggested were:

- *Step-sister not to go in my room when I am not there.*
- *Bedtimes should be the same.*
- *To have the same pocket money.*
- *Spend equal amount of time with Mum as her step-sister spends with Dad.*

The rules child two suggested were:

- *To be allowed biscuits or crisps at the weekend as her step-sister is allowed them.*
- *To continue to stay up to see Dad when he comes home late from work.*
- *To be able to use the computer every day after she has finished her homework.*

I took both sets of rules and showed them to the parents and said, 'This is what both of your children would like to happen. Please have a look at them and see which rules you could enforce.' The whole family had a meeting and the rules going forward were placed in the kitchen for everyone to see.

Finally, children want and need to learn how to resolve conflict on their own. It is a life skill that they can use in later years in relationships and in a work environment. By doing something as simple as the actions above they will learn how to resolve conflicts on their own. They will also get to understand the needs of others, have the ability to listen well and learn how their actions affect other children.

Checklist

- Sibling rivalry is normal and healthy.
- Spend one-to-one time with your children every day if possible.

- Teach your children to share and negotiate.
- Highlight to them why sometimes you have to treat them differently.
- Don't intervene in arguments too early.
- Teach your children to respect each other's space and property.

chapter eight

How to help your child through family breakdown

'Whatever brawls disturb the street, there should be peace at home'   ISAAC WATTS

Parent separation

When parents separate it can be an incredibly traumatic time for children. They can feel that their world, their security and the stability that they have always known has fallen apart. The experience is a hugely emotional one where they have so many different feelings running through their bodies at the same time, as they have to get their head around living with one parent instead of the two they are used to. They may worry that their parents don't love them any more; they can feel abandoned, anxious, very scared and insecure. They may even feel that it is their fault.

In this chapter I want to address some of the fears and worries that children have. I cannot address all of them so I am going to concentrate on the main ones that children come to see me about and give you some handy hints of what you can say to your child in each instance. In all the examples and language used in this chapter I have assumed that the parents' separation is not due to physical abuse and that either parent could have made the decision to break up the marriage or partnership.

Talking it through

One of the most important things to happen when you separate is to get your child to talk to you. It can be hard to get your child to open up at the best of times, but when you are going through parent separation it can be more difficult, especially if your child sees the break-up as your fault. Talking, though, is essential. Children need to communicate how they feel about the situation so that you can help them manage and understand their feelings. There will be lots of changes going on in their lives.

Your child will feel more able to open up to you if you make and spend quality time with them.

THE TOOL TO USE

Talking about it tool

1 Find a time to talk to your child one to one – perhaps it could be a car journey or while making dinner.

2 Talk to them about their feelings and thoughts and acknowledge them. With each feeling that they mention, ask them what makes them feel that way. How together could you make that feeling disappear? What could you do as a parent to help them? What are their biggest fears? What do they need from you?

3 Share some of your feelings with them. Your children need to know that you have feelings, too, about the separation.

4 Use words like, 'I am sad that Dad and I cannot live together any more,' and 'We will still love you and we will worry that you are okay.'

5 Explain to them that this change affects all family members and that together you will be learning and having to adjust to this new situation, too.

See Chapter 6 for more detailed suggestions on how to talk about fears and for ways to help your child cope with them.

This quality time may also include books. Show them books about family break-ups so that they can learn what to expect when it happens. If your child does not read well get them a picture book and talk about what they see as well as you reading the story to them. There are so many books in the library and in bookshops that talk about what you can expect if your parents split up, and they are for all age groups. Using books will bring your child and the situation closer and it will help your child understand that they are not the first person to go through this life change. Other people have done so and been okay.

Your children will want to understand what is going on. They will ask you lots of questions and may repeat the same ones over and over again so they can become clear as to the situation. When you answer you don't need to give them a full-blown account of why the break-up occurred and who was to blame. Just give them enough information as they need to understand. For example, 'Mum and Dad have not been getting on very well. You may have heard us arguing. We all want to be happy but Mum and Dad find that they are not happy living in the same house, therefore Dad has decided to live somewhere else. Dad/Mum is going to live around the corner. You will still see him/her and spend time with him/her but he/she just won't be living in this house.' Another way of explaining is by saying, 'When Mum and Dad got together they were quite young and as we have got older we have realised we have both changed and in a way have fallen out of love with each other. We still love you and always will but we have decided together, Dad and I, that we would be happier not living together.'

When you talk to your child use language that is age relevant. The above examples may not be right for a child who is aware of what's been going on and understands more about the complexities of relationships. I think in all cases that children need to know that you have tried to make things right so that in later years they know that it is important to work at a relationship when it is not going right and that walking away is not an option that should be taken lightly.

Whose fault is it?

Children fear that it is their fault unless they are told it isn't, so tell them! As I mentioned above, if you give them the right information they need they will know that it isn't.

An example of this type of anxiety was shown in Callum, who had been in trouble at school, to the extent his mum and dad had been called into the school about his behaviour. He was really upset about his parents being called in and modified his behaviour. However, when his parents split up several weeks later he felt that it was his fault – he had caused them to separate. He believed if only he had 'behaved well at school' it may not have happened. After discussing his 'irrational thought' he decided to tell his mum that he thought he was the cause of the break-up. She was relieved that he had admitted his feelings and explained to him that it was just a coincidence that the two situations had happened at the same time. She told him that she and his dad had not been getting on very well for a long time and that they could not live and be happy together any more. That explanation really helped Callum.

For Sarah the situation was different. Her mum and dad had been bickering for weeks on end and they had decided that her dad would move out for a trial separation. In order for her dad to go without the children around, they decided that Sarah and her brother would stay over at a friend's house one Saturday night. Dad could then move some of his things out of the house unnoticed and without hundreds of questions thrown at him by the children. Sarah said goodbye to her parents and went off to her friend's house while her mum spent a stressful evening 'moving out Dad'.

When Sarah returned the following day her mum explained to her why her dad was not at home. Sarah could not understand that in 24 hours she had had an amazing sleepover at her friend's while her dad had moved out of the family home. What did that mean? Yes, Mum and Dad had been arguing but why did Dad go so quickly and why did it happen when she was not there? What had she and her brother done? Mum explained to her that she wanted Dad to go on a positive note and that this was the way that Mum and Dad thought would be easiest for her and her brother. Sarah disagreed because she would have preferred to say goodbye to her dad. I worked with Sarah on lots of

> *different issues surrounding her parents' separation, mainly to give her a greater understanding of what was happening in all their lives and why.*

What is going to happen to your child?

Whenever you are talking about the separation give your child the reassurance that everyone that is part of the family is going to go through this major lifestyle change together and that you are going to try and keep their life as similar as you possibly can. That means staying at the same school, doing the same after school activities, etc., and encourage them to do what they have always done as much as possible. Of course there will be some changes such as they will be living with one parent and seeing the other one at other times, but hopefully their stability in attending school and being surrounded by their friends will stay the same.

In extreme cases both parents will have to move house and your child, regardless of the parent they are living with, may have to leave old friends behind. Friends play a big part of their security and so they will still need to see them. Just as you will want and need to spend time with your friends, so too will your children. If your child says that they feel lonely or they are worried about losing touch with their friends ask them how would they like to keep in touch with them, what would they and their friends prefer?

Talk to them about going to visit old friends and suggest to them that now might be a good time to make use of social websites such as Facebook, email, MSN, SKYPE and texts to stay in contact with them if appropriate. These are all inexpensive but effective ways of keeping old friendships going and it can be comforting for your child to know that at a touch of a button they can reach out to a friend for help, advice or just to let off steam.

Feelings

Some children will worry about the situation and what is going to happen next. It can make them feel anxious and stressed. If you notice that your child is worried or they tell you that they are worried talk to them about it. Do they know what they could do to make them feel less stressed and worried?

I asked this question to a nine-year-old girl called Charlie and we managed to come up with some great answers between us.

- *Do some exercise. She said jumping on the trampoline or running around the garden lots of times made her feel good afterwards. I asked her why it made her feel good and she said it gave her a chance to think about the situation. Exercise is a* great stress buster, it can help children process their thoughts and get rid of any negative feelings.

- *Relax.* Charlie said she liked to watch TV to relax as it made her think about something else. I asked her, 'What other ways could you use to relax?' She said listening to music or making something. I suggested relaxation techniques and imagery. She quite liked the sound of both of them but said she would have to try them out first.

  If your child is willing to try out some relaxation techniques, there are some in Chapter 7.

- *Write it down.* If Charlie wrote down her worries in a notebook the worries would stay on the paper and not in her head. (It really can work, especially if you tell your child that is what happens.) I also suggested to her that since she likes to be creative she could draw some pictures of how she feels.

  Your child may not want to talk to you about everything they feel, especially if it is about you, so writing it down or drawing it out is a happy medium. They can even keep the notebook and drawings somewhere safe where you can't find it. I think giving children control, especially in circumstances such as these, having a diary and keeping it in a secret place can make them feel better and more powerful.

- *Talk. Charlie suggested that if she talked to someone about the way she felt she would feel less stressed. She was talking to me and felt much better because she could say whatever she liked and those thoughts and feelings were kept safe in my house.*

  If you know your child is unhappy and they refuse to talk to you (you may be the baddy) explain to them the benefits of talking to someone they trust with their feelings such as a teacher, family friend, counsellor or therapist. Children can have such strong feelings and they should not have to cope with some of them on their own. I always think a problem shared takes away some of the weight upon their shoulders.

- *Find out how others coped. I suggested to Charlie that another idea might be for her to talk to someone in her class at school whose parents have gone through the same thing so that they could share experiences of their mum and dad splitting up. They could ask their classmate how they felt when their parents split up. What did they do? Who did they talk to and what is life like for them now?*

After discussing and writing down the above suggestions Charlie decided to try out the diary idea and when she felt stressed she would go outside and run around the garden – sometimes kicking a ball around to get more stress out.

What ideas would you suggest to your child so that they worry less and feel less stressed?

Some of the stress that children carry may be about themselves, or it may be about the people they love around them. They may be worried about you and how you are coping. They may be worried that Mum or Dad is lonely and has nothing to do when they are not there. Children are very perceptive and will easily pick up on how you are feeling. They can sense it in your tone of voice and your mood. You are allowed to be sad or thoughtful – just be careful what you say, how you say it and how you act around them. It is better to be strong around them rather than crying and not wanting to get up, get dressed and be there for them.

If your child thinks you are lonely it will make them feel guilty and sad and they will want to 'parent' you rather than the other way around. If they ask you about being lonely let them know that you aren't and tell them that when they aren't there you have so many other things that you can do. Share with them all those jobs and chores.

Money

For most parents splitting up it will be inevitable that one or both of you will end up with a smaller house or even a flat. Some parents have to go back to renting or sharing a flat with other people because the divorce process is just so expensive. It is likely your child will be worried that one parent has to live in a smaller place while the other parent gets the family home. If your child is asking you questions about housing arrangements explain to them that when you were all living together the money that was coming into the house was paying for the mortgage, bills, food and doing nice things for all of you. Now this money has to be split in half.

Can they imagine the house being split in two – how many bedrooms would it have and how much 'living' room would there be? If they realise that half a house is two bedrooms and one 'living' room and half a garden they will understand more that this is all your money will buy or rent when you live apart. This all makes sense to a child until they see that one parent is still living in the family home and the other parent is living in a much smaller place, then it makes no sense at all.

So how do you explain Mum or Dad getting the house

and the other parent living in less-dignified accommodation than they are used to? It is not easy to explain as each 'parent separation' situation is going to be different. No matter what you tell your child they are going to think it is unfair. I think the best way to approach this is to say that the decision of where Mum and Dad were going to live was a choice you made together and that the parent who is moving to a smaller place chose to. Don't suggest to them that it was the other parent's idea.

One of the frustrating things for children occurs when they are visiting their 'other parent in the smaller accommodation'. Several children have said to me in a coaching session, 'I want more room for my clothes and toys' or 'I don't want to have to sleep in the lounge or have to share a bedroom with all my siblings.' They also tell me that they are too scared to ask Mum or Dad for more space or a better sleeping arrangement because they know they don't have it.

There are lots of children who are too afraid of asking their parents questions about the separation because they do not want to upset their parent. Some children will worry about how you are living and if there is enough money for you to eat, if you will have enough food when they stay with you to feed you both, pay bills and have money to do activities with them. Your child may even offer to give you some money so that you don't go hungry. Don't take offence as they are only trying to help.

Give them the reassurance that there is enough money for the basics but you may not be able to afford to go out for dinner when they come to stay all the time. Explain to them regardless of parent separation, there are going to be times for parents when there is very little money because of other priorities such as rent, bills, petrol, etc. If you don't share these priorities with your child they will not understand the reason why you aren't doing something fabulous every time you see them. Talking to them about what money has to be used for will also teach them about responsibility and the value of money. You could have a conversation with them like this:

'Now that Mum and Dad are not living together any more we both have less money. My money has to pay for rent, bills, food, etc. and I also give some to Mum/Dad so that you have school uniforms, food and money for school trips. If I gave you £100 and you had to pay £50 for rent, £15 for bills, £10 for food and £10 for Mum or Dad, how much would you have left and what would you spend it on?' I wonder what they would say.

It can be hard for a child to get used to the idea of their parents living apart so make it clear that this new arrangement will become normal life. It is not a holiday or special occasion whenever they stay with the other parent and so they shouldn't always expect treats or outings. After all, they probably didn't go to theme parks every week when their parents were together.

New rules

Another issue that really frustrates children is the change of rules. It is very possible that after Mum or Dad leaves the house rules change. There may be stricter rules or they may be more lax. Mum may carry on being strict and Dad may decide to throw all rules out of the window.

Children, however much they hate rules, know that they are good for them and they make them feel secure and safe. Having two sets of rules, though, can be very confusing for some children. For instance, they may be allowed to stay up late at the weekends with one parent but then the following weekend with the other parent they have to be in bed as usual by 8pm. And they will protest – always against the parent who does not let them stay up late.

If you can, please agree between you on some mutual, consistent rules. Bedtimes and what they are allowed to eat are two very good ones. I think these two are the ones that most of the children I see complain about. If you do decide to become stricter discuss the new rules and boundaries with your child so they know what they have to comply to and give them some time to adjust to the new rules. They may forget about them from time to time. If they do, gently remind them by saying, 'New rules' or 'Not in my house.'

Children welcome the idea of being involved in the discussions about the new rules so if you can ask them what they would like some of the new rules to be. They also like to have input into the changes in lifestyle that are going to occur and parent visitation. Even though adults have the final say, children feel valued when their wishes are heard and taken into consideration. Perhaps your child would like to spend every weekend with their mum or dad rather than every other or maybe they would like the option of staying over at their home on a Wednesday night because they have a sleepover at a friend's on the Saturday. Could you be flexible?

It is the same for decisions. Children feel more secure if they are allowed to continue making some of their own decisions and if they are given a choice. By letting them choose what they want to eat, to wear or how to spend their allowance, it will help them to feel that they do have some control over their life, which in turn will help eliminate their feeling of helplessness. They will feel helpless because they know that there is nothing they can do to bring their family back together, but they will often hope that it will happen someday and cling on to that thought.

Separation can be final

What do you do when your child repeatedly asks you when their mum or dad is going to come back home? It is a difficult one, especially when you know that there is usually only one answer: they're not. Your child clearly does not register that the separation is final and so I think it is important to ask them a few questions to help them to start to think about the reality of Mum and Dad being apart. I would ask them, 'What do you think would happen if we stayed together? Would you want us to be upset and angry with each other and be unhappy? Have you wanted to be in the house when we have not been "normal" around each other? How did you feel hearing us argue or shout because we don't want to live together any more?' Get them to imagine a situation where there is noise, stress or shouting and ask them how they would feel. Now get them to think of Mum and Dad living in different places and returning home from school with no uneasy atmosphere, etc. How do they feel now? Talk through the two different feelings. I am sure they would prefer the second scenario despite the hurt that they are feeling.

Ellen wanted her parents back together. She couldn't understand why they could not just make up. After all, when she and her friends fall out they say sorry and get their friendship back on track. If she could move on with her friends then surely her parents could do the same. Ellen felt a real need to know why her parents had split up and why they had to live apart permanently. She wanted to hear this from both parents so I suggested to her parents that they did this together. Before they had this conversation I asked Ellen if she thought it was a good idea to make a list of questions that she could ask her parents while they were both in the same room. She thought it was. Ellen had the conversation with her parents and it gave her the peace of mind she needed along with the answers she had not received before.

Handover

Your children may not mention this to you but they can often feel awkward and insecure during the handing over process from one parent to the other. They want the transition to be smooth and to hear civil words spoken, but sometimes children hear things they probably shouldn't. If you are going to talk about what happened during the visit, children would prefer it if you spoke about it after the handover and when they are out of earshot. Whispering, low voices or asking your child to leave the room so you can discuss how their weekend was can make your child feel awkward and also make them feel that you are hiding something.

When you are together moving your child, from one parent to the other, think about how they feel saying goodbye to one parent and hello to the other. Seeing you both together may make them feel sad but it can soften the blow if they see you behaving well and being civil towards each other when they are around.

What is the one thing you could do to make the handover seamless?

Piggy in the middle

Where does a child lay their loyalty when it comes to Mum and Dad? They shouldn't have to choose which parent to side with, but they can sometimes find themselves doing so because of what one parent has said or done. For example, one parent may have been having an affair or one parent may have been repeatedly verbally abusive to the other.

Trying to make your children take sides or turn them against the other parent intentionally, places them in the middle of an adult struggle and really that is not the place where they want to be. Children generally want to make both their parents happy and want to be loyal to both so don't make them choose.

It is very tempting to say to your child, 'I can't wait for the divorce to be over so I don't have to speak to your mum/dad again' or moan about the other parent for not doing something. Don't complain about the other parent as your child won't want to hear – they just aren't interested. It is also very tempting to question your child about what the other parent is doing in their life or who they like the best. If you feel like you are going to ask them a question like this, stop yourself! Focus on what you are doing in your own life and when your child is in your custody focus on the activity you are doing together and on them.

> *One of my clients, Daisy, did not like it when she returned from staying with her dad at the weekend as her mum would bombard her with questions about what she did, what she ate, who she saw, what her dad bought her. Daisy would tell her mum everything but felt guilty about having such a great time with her dad. She wanted to be honest and not upset her mum but her mum was probing her – what else could she do? I asked Daisy if she could change the situation in any way so that she did not feel uncomfortable talking about her time with her dad. She said, 'Yes, I would like to tell Mum not to ask me questions and volunteer the information – as much or as little as I would want.' We spoke to her mum together and they agreed to try out this new idea in the future.*

Children don't want to be put in awkward situations. Think about what you are saying to your child and consider, 'Should I be telling them this? Should I be asking this question and am I being fair to them?' You need to be neutral and non-judgemental about the other parent when your child asks you about them.

Be strong and focus on what your child needs to hear that will enable them to continue to respect their other parent. For example, 'Dad should not have done that, but you had a good time so let's forget about it', rather than, 'Your father has no idea how to look after you.'

Another way you can put your child in the middle is to use them to convey messages between you both so you don't actually have to speak directly to the other parent. A young child will be willing to do this because they want to please the parent giving the message and it can make them feel important. An older child will probably feel resentful that Mum and Dad cannot actually talk to each other.

More often than not, though, your child won't like being the messenger. They would rather you talked directly to each other so that messages are communicated in a clear way and not potentially misinterpreted. It is a big responsibility for your child to remember the correct and whole message. It is a bit like a game children love to play where you have to whisper something to another person and then they whisper it to someone else. The message often gets distorted. I think it is best kept as a game for children.

It does not show a great example to your children and it is unfair to your child to carry messages to your 'ex' because you find it too awkward or aggravating to do so yourself. It can also imply to your child that the other parent is such a monster that you cannot speak or be civil to them.

Wherever possible, communicate directly with the other parent about matters relevant to your children, such as when they are going to see them, health issues and school matters. If you cannot speak with them directly in the right tone then use email or instant messenger. Try and remember that you were good communicators in the past and for your children's sake try and do this again.

What can you do differently, that is also realistic, so that your child is not used as a messenger?

Step-families

It can be really hard for children when you have two families coming together especially when the children are used to family life being just Mum and their siblings. The children not only have to adjust to a new person or new people being a part of the household, but they may also have different rules and living conditions. The children I see in this situation tend to find having more rules and having to share their parent or their things with the other children the most challenging. For some step-families, though, it is a wonderful experience – more children to play with and a new parent who is nothing like their other parent. It can be a refreshing change. I am not going to focus on the children who embrace their new family because I don't see them. This section focuses on how you can help your child if they aren't finding step-family life as easy as it could be.

I worked with a step-family where the children were very confused about the rules of the 'new household'. The children found it very difficult to get on as both sets of children were treated differently by their respective parents and the rules were different for both sides of the family. I had four unhappy children. I asked all of them what life was like before they all moved in together. Were there any rules and what were they? What were the rules they were expected to follow now? What did they disagree with regarding the rules? I also asked them what they needed from their birth parent that they were living with and what they wanted to happen with regards to the way they were being treated by their step-parent.

All the children agreed that, as well as having the same ground rules, they felt they needed their own space and needed their step-siblings to respect that. They felt that they should be treated fairly and both parents should follow the same level of strictness. Another point that came up was that the children did not feel they knew enough about each other and thought it might help if they did. They had come to live together quite quickly and had not had much time to get to know each other's personalities.

The children needed to spend time with each other talking about what they liked, disliked, what they enjoyed doing in their spare time and their interests. They also needed to communicate to each other about what kind of person they were – did they get up early in the morning? When are they happy and grumpy? What personal space did they need, if any?

With children who are not used to living with each other under the same roof, this kind of information is important. I got them to talk to each other and they took it in turns to say something about themselves. This exercise gave them a better understanding of each other's needs and wants, which in turn got them to get along with each other.

There are other exercises you can do if you find you need to break the ice and get your children to get to know their new step-siblings. Why not get everyone to write down a profile of themselves and mix them all up – each person takes one and then has to guess who it is. Another idea is get all the children to write down something they like about each other and then share it with their siblings. Compliments from those we don't expect them from make us feel great.

Once the children felt that they knew each other better we started talking about the rules. I asked them collectively which rules they would like and we wrote them down on a huge piece of paper. After collating them all, I asked both 'parents' to join us and we sat down as a family to discuss and negotiate them. The rules were around bedtimes, chores, one-to-one time with their own parent, who was allowed to discipline whom, punishments and rewards. We had to come up with viable and realistic rules that would work for everyone, but were not too far away from the children who were not used to much discipline and not too lax for the others who were used to a level of strictness. It took some time but over the period of weeks the children started to adjust to their new rules and new family.

If you are part of a step-family and you can see your child rebelling against being part of it, speak to them and ask them what would they like to change that is within their power? Do they feel that they are making an effort with the 'new arrivals'? What could they do to make life easier for everyone else?

There are lots of niggles when it comes to step-families, especially around rules. What if your child is used to having lots of freedom and now their step-parent does not allow them to cycle to their friends' on their own or let them cross roads alone? Once you have empowered your child and given them some responsibility it is very difficult to take it away.

> *I worked with a boy called Richard who did not end up living with step-siblings, but his mum moved her boyfriend in. The boyfriend had no experience of children so it was very difficult for him to discipline Richard. He did not know what he was doing and therefore when he felt that Richard was not behaving in a correct manner he would make him go to his room. Clearly Richard did not agree with how he was disciplined. He said he would rather his mum was left to discipline him or the boyfriend gave him a warning first and a fair punishment if he continued to do something wrong. I asked Richard how he could approach this. Could he speak to his mum or the boyfriend about this? He said he would prefer to speak to his mum. What would he say and when could he discuss it with her? He said he would tell her how he felt and what he wanted to happen in the future. He would discuss this with her when they were next alone. He discussed the situation with his mum and, together with the boyfriend, they came up with a new set of discipline rules.*

If you are going to let your new partner discipline your child it is always helpful to tell them what already works and how you would like them to use discipline. A crash course in parenting is needed if you are going to share the parenting.

> Who is allowed to discipline your child and how do you want them to be disciplined?

Does not like Step-dad or Step-mum

A young girl called Zoe, aged eight, came to see me because she did not like her step-dad. I asked her why and we made a list of the things she did not like. I then asked her to make a list of all the good things about him. Once we had the two lists I asked her if she wanted to get on better with him – 'Yes', she replied. I asked her what did 'getting on better' mean to her? She said she wanted to be able to talk to him like she talked to her dad. She said she wanted to have a conversation with him but found the things that she did not like about him got in the way. Here is her list of what she did not like about her step-dad:

- *He does not help around the house.*
- *He makes her tidy her room.*
- *He sings loudly.*

- *He does not let her watch her favourite TV programme.*

We worked our way down the list and decided if she could do anything to change his 'annoying' habits. She could see that there were solutions to most of them and for those that she could not change she would have to adjust her thinking about them. For example, she could not change the fact that he does not help around the house but she could speak to Mum and ask her to talk to him about letting her watch her favourite TV programme. When Zoe put the good and the bad into perspective she realised that her step-dad was not that bad and could actually see the situation getting better.

So could she have a conversation with him now? If so, what, when and how? This is how the rest of our conversation went:

Me: *'When could you talk to him?'*

Zoe: *'At dinnertime.'*

Me: *'Is it possible to do it at this time?'*

Zoe: *'Yes, Mum and her boyfriend have dinner together.'*

Me: *'Could you join them?'*

Zoe: *'Yes.'*

Me: *'What would you talk about?'*

Zoe: *'I would ask him about his day.'*

The following week I saw Zoe and she said her week had been better and her mum had noticed she had made an effort with her step-dad.

Zoe is not the only child who has had an issue with her step-parent.

Mia found that when she was having an argument with her dad, her step-mum would often interfere. Mia would get annoyed. After talking through the options of what Mia could do to stop her step-mum interfering, Mia decided she would speak to her dad and ask him to speak to her step-mum about not getting involved. I asked her when she would do this and she said the next time she was alone with him. The following session when we reviewed the progress she said she had spoken to her dad and he had promised her he would speak to his wife about not getting involved. Following up in a phone call with Mia, she said that she and her step-mum were getting on better as she was no longer getting involved in the disagreements Mia had with her dad – result!

Checklist

- Answer all your child's questions and use age-relevant language.
- Make time to talk.

- Keep your child's routine as 'normal' as possible.

- Money issues worry children.

- Piggy in the middle is a children's game.

- Parent as a unit even when you are apart.

- Revisit rules and discipline when becoming a step-family.

chapter nine

How to help your child deal with school issues

*'**Bully**: A person who uses strength or influence to harm or intimidate those who are weaker'*   OXFORD DICTIONARY

Bullying

Sad to say, but very true, bullying is everywhere. As parents we can experience it at work, in the school playground, among other parents or with our neighbours. It does not matter how old we are, bullying is uncalled for and unnecessary. Children often think that they cannot stop the bullies. In some ways they are right as we cannot change the behaviour of others. Bullies are responsible for their own actions. What we can teach our children is how to respond better to the bullies. Bullying can be physical, verbal, racist or emotional and it can completely knock a child's self-confidence and self-esteem. It can be done online via social networking sites or other social media. Cyber-bullying is rife due to the bullies not having to look their victim in the eye, giving them the confidence to say whatever they like to their victim. If your child is old enough to be using a social networking site talk to them about online bullying and make them aware of what they should do if they see anything abusive (e.g. block and report the bullies). Suggest to your child that they only friend the people they know and trust – including you, so you can keep a tab on their activity from time to time.

Before I carry on I would like to make a point. In this chapter we are going to talk about standard playground bullying, such as hurtful teasing and physical annoyance. This is the level of bullying experienced by most of the children who come to my clinic. More extreme situations need to be dealt with by the school, so make sure you know your child's school bullying policy.

Why do children bully?

Some children do it to hide their own inadequacy (i.e. because they do not feel great about themselves). They can have low self-esteem and feel insecure about who they are. They don't want to face up to the fact that their life is not that great and they are unhappy, so they project their inadequacy on to other children. Children can also bully because they want to hide who they are really are.

A bully may never have learnt that they need to accept responsibility for their behaviour. They may not even be able to recognise the effect of their bullying on other children, which is why they continue to do it and they may not know any other way of behaving. Children who bully may have seen other people do it and see the sense of power it can bring and want to be like them. They may also come from a background where that behaviour is not only acceptable, but normal!

There are so many reasons behind why a bully bullies and I think it is important that you convey all the possibilities to your child. They need to understand that not all children are brought up in the same way as them and that those children's parents may not parent in the same way as you. Bullies often have a wide range of prejudices as a reason to dump their anger on to others. They can be driven by jealousy, envy and even rejection.

Bullying can really affect your child's moods, sleep pattern, appetite and enthusiasm for life. Many children worry about going to school for fear of the bullies or for getting into trouble themselves.

Christopher, for example, was upset because Morgan used to call him names every day and he found it difficult to sleep at night. I saw Christopher during the school holidays and we chatted about Morgan. Christopher was already thinking about going back to school and getting worried about seeing Morgan again. I asked him if it was worth him worrying when instead he should be relaxing and having fun with his other friends. He said, 'No.'

I asked Christopher what else he could do to stop worrying about something that had not happened yet. Perhaps Morgan has changed and may not call him names any more. What else could he think so that Morgan did not ruin his school holidays?

- *'It is my school holidays and I am going to enjoy it.'*
- *'I am more important than Morgan.'*
- *'How do I know Morgan is going to be horrible? I may be worrying about nothing.'*
- *'If Morgan picks on me I now have lots of ideas of what I am going to do.' His ideas were to be nice to him even if Morgan was horrible and also to tell the teacher. As Morgan was always in trouble he felt that the teacher would believe him.*

Christopher changed his thought process so he could enjoy the rest of the holidays and felt more positive about returning to school.

Responding to the bullies

If your child says that they are being bullied discuss with them why they think they are. Some children can perceive that they are a victim of bullying when a friend unintentionally ignores them, someone jokes around with them or they are not invited to join in a game. All of these can hurt your child's feelings and it can be very upsetting for them. Their friend may not have said or done something to your child maliciously or even know that they have done something wrong, but if your child is hurt by the words or the actions then you need to talk to them about it.

It is important that we listen to our children when they say that they are being bullied. Bullying is an intentional act to provoke and anger others. You know your child and their temperament. If they are saying they are being bullied but from their explanation you can tell that the actions of the other child were not on purpose but your child has perceived them to be intentional, explain the difference to them between their friends having a joke/teasing them and bullying. Then you can help them address the problem in the correct way. Both make children feel unhappy and both are unkind and unfair.

If your child is being bullied there are many things you can do to work with your child so that the bullying stops. Obviously there are different degrees of bullying so one idea may work better than another. I would discuss all these ideas with them and see how many they would like to try out:

- Teach them how to look assertive – maintain eye contact with the bullies and use strong body language. By strong body language, I mean standing tall, shoulders back and feeling strong like they are going to take on Goliath. Get them to walk around the room like this so they can get the stance right.

- Get them to speak up. If the bully says something to them, they can say something back. Perhaps they could stick to the same phrase, such as, 'I will not let you beat me' or 'Leave me alone'. Teach them to not rise to the bait and to give as good as they receive.
- Teach them positive self-talk. Essentially, they can say to themselves, 'I am good. I am kind. I don't care what they say' and walk off.
- If they can, get them to hide their emotions. If the bully says something horrible expecting to get a reaction from them they will be disappointed that they didn't and they may leave them alone.
- Your child could stop the bully in their tracks when the bully says something derogatory like, 'You're stupid' and your child responds with, 'Thank you' or 'I know'. There is no comeback.
- They could speak to their teacher to make them aware of the situation.
- They could walk away and join another group of friends at break times.
- Your child could get all of their feelings about the bully down on paper. They could write a note to themselves if they find it hard to tell you how they are feeling about it all. They could also keep a diary of what kind of bullying

is happening and when it is occurring. This can be used as 'evidence' if and when they need to take the matter further.

Support your child as much as they need you to and work together as a team with the teachers and the school to eradicate the situation.

Knowing your child as you do, how do you think they would stop the bullies and what support do you think they would need from you?

Sally, aged seven, came to see me as she felt that she was being bullied. A group of girls in her class were calling her names, following her and making up lies about her. Sally and I got stuck into how we could change the situation straightaway. We made a list of how she could protect herself and her feelings from the actions of the girls and graded each idea in the list. One was the worst thing to do and 10 was the best. As we graded them Sally told me if she thought there would be any repercussions to each action. In other words, would anything bad happen. The options were:

- *Ask them to stop – 4/10.*
- *Walk away – 6/10.*
- *Ask them why they do it – 3/10.*
- *Pretend it is funny – 1/10.*
- *Tell the teacher – 5/10.*
- *Explain how she feels to the girls – 10/10.*
- *Ignore them – 5/10.*

With regards to the name calling, Sally chose to be honest with the girls and tell them how she felt. She felt the repercussions of telling them were fairly limited. The worst they would do was to laugh at her and the best outcome was that the girls would understand how she felt. Perhaps they did not even realise the name-calling was upsetting her. If that was the case they may understand how upset Sally was and be kinder to her. If they did not respond to her honesty then she decided she should go and play with her other friends. When it came to the lies and following her around Sally decided she would walk away and ignore the girls. With a conversation on how great Sally was, she realised she was worth more than the way she was being treated.

The following week when we saw each other again she said the walking off was working and when she confronted the girls about the name calling one of the girls apologised to her and had started being kinder. She felt happier and hoped over time her resilience to the name calling and them getting bored by a lack of response would wane and then stop.

THE TOOL TO USE

Stop bullying tool

1 If your child comes to you saying they are being bullied and they want to stop it themselves make a list together of how they could stop the bullying.

2 Ask them what they think would happen if they carried out each action to stop the bullying.

3 Ask them if the action would make the situation any better or if it would make it worse?

4 Ask your child to give each idea a mark out of 10 – 10 being the best.

5 Get them to try out their idea.

6 Monitor the situation over a period of weeks by getting your child's feedback.

7 If the idea is working for them get them to continue. If your child feels that they can still handle the situation themselves and wants to try out another idea let them.

6 If your child feels the bullying situation has gone too far talk about school intervention. In the meantime work with your child to make them feel stronger about the situation and themselves.

Josh's mum was concerned that Josh was being bullied because he was coming home from school and not wanting to talk about his day. When I questioned him about the change in his behaviour at home he said there were a couple of boys in his class that were being unkind to him. In lessons they would pull his hair and prod him in the back and in the playground they would call him names. He wanted it to stop but he did not want his parents or teachers to get involved. I asked him if it was okay to mention to his mum what was going on. He said yes but he wanted to handle it himself so we made a list of the actions Josh wanted to take in order to stop the bullying:

- *Say something to the boys that would make them stop in their tracks – 8/10.*
- *Look less scared and walk away if in the playground. If in the classroom ask the teacher if he could move places – 5/10.*
- *Retaliate and fight back – 3/10.*
- *Stay with his friends and build a unity so the bullies could not get to him – 8/10.*

I made lots of suggestions but Josh wanted to focus on his ideas. I asked him what did he think would happen if he did any of the above? He felt that on reflection the second option would not work as the boys would probably follow him and his retaliation idea could make the situation worse. He thought if he said something back to the boys, they would be stunned and that could be a good thing. He also thought that his unity idea of having 'bodyguards' may put off the bullies so that they would leave him alone. Josh gave each idea a mark out of 10 which cemented his decision to try out his first and last ideas. I saw him a week later and he said the boys had not been so bad but that may have been because a couple of them had been away. I then saw him two weeks later and he said the boys had started again and that he wanted the problem to go away quickly. I asked him what that meant and he said he wanted to tell the teacher and get his mum involved. Josh and his mum spoke to the school and I continued to work with Josh on his self-esteem, explaining that it was not his fault that the bullying had happened.

Mean to others

Why is your child being mean to others? That is a question that they may not want to answer but all the same if you have another parent or child telling you that your child is being mean you will want to get to the bottom of it. Who are they being mean to and why? Ask your child how they would feel if someone was being mean to them. Would they like it? Can they think of how they would like to be seen by others? What could your child do to change? Talk to them about control and holding back on following others around or saying something horrible. Get them to think, 'If I am kind then people will like me' and realise that if they do not start to change they are going to be sad and lonely. If your child is being mean to others they may be lacking in a healthy self-esteem. They may not feel great about themselves and therefore feel the need to make others feel bad to make themselves feel better (see Chapter 8 to help raise your child's self-esteem).

Concentration

Not every child finds it easy to concentrate. Lessons may be boring and so their mind wanders or they get distracted by the person sitting next to them. Children think that it is okay not to pay attention but it can have an impact on them later on in life if they don't.

It can be a vicious cycle:

> If I don't listen ... I don't know what to do ... I will have to do the work slowly ... the teacher will tell me off ... I don't like the teacher ... so I don't listen.

A cycle that needs to be broken

Parents may be worried about the academic success of a child and therefore contact me to help them with their concentration skills. I explain to the child about the importance of lessons. I ask them what they want to do when they leave school – what would be their perfect job? What would they have to do to get there? It is likely they will need to pass some exams and they can only do this if they concentrate and participate in the classroom.

I will find out what makes the lesson boring and I probe them to find something good about it. I also suggest to them that perhaps they could think to themselves, 'If I do not pay attention I will be in trouble or I will not get the grades I want.'

It can be hard for children to bring their attention back to the classroom when their mind wanders. They could say to themselves, 'Right now I need to work. I can mess around later outside of class.' If they do have someone putting them off learning in lessons perhaps they could ask the teacher if they can move desks, ignore the distractors or think, 'I need to concentrate otherwise I will not know what the homework is and I won't be able to do it.'

Tim always got into trouble because he did not concentrate in class. He ended up in detention regularly and his parents had received a letter home about his behaviour at school. The next step after having a letter sent home was going on report which Tim clearly did not want to happen. The reason that he got into trouble was because the other children in his class would throw things at him during lessons and so in retaliation he would throw something back at them. I asked Tim if he had any ideas of what he could do to stop this from happening. He said, 'Don't throw anything back.' How could he back this up with his positive thoughts? He could think to himself, 'I must not throw anything back otherwise I will be grounded and I don't want that to happen.' What could he do with the items thrown at him? Well he could keep them until the end of the lesson and then hand them back to the perpetrators. It worked; he actually did this. He did not throw anything back despite the boys throwing things at him and he gave them back the items. The boys were shocked and after a few days they got bored and gave up.

Scheduling

Some children find it really hard to fit everything into their life, especially after school when they have tutors, activities, homework and they also want and need to relax. Devising a homework plan (see page 234) will certainly help your child be more organised with their work. But what about your child's routine after school? I have had many children sit in front of me and complain that when they return from school they have to do their homework straightaway and they don't want to. Would they prefer to have a drink and something to eat after school before they start their homework or do they want to watch TV then do homework after dinner? What do they do when they have an after school activity and have to find time to do their homework? When can they do it? What is going to work best for them? Not all children are the same when it comes to an after school routine, so decide on a plan together. Warning – negotiation may be needed here!

Here's what an after school activity plan may look like:

AFTER SCHOOL ACTIVITY PLAN

Monday	Tuesday	Wednesday	Thursday	Friday
Home and snack	After school club	Home and snack	After school club	Home and snack
Homework	Home and relax	Homework	Homework	Free time
Dinner	Dinner	Dinner	Dinner	Dinner
Scouts	Homework	Tutor	Home	Free time
Relax	Relax	Relax	Relax	Relax
8.30pm Bed	8.30pm Bed	8.30pm Bed	8.30pm Bed	9pm Bed

What would your child's after school plan look like?

Secondary school transition

Starting secondary school can be an anxious time for your child. There's a new teacher for them to meet, new work, old friends they didn't want to see again after primary school and the scary thought that they are going to meet a whole bunch of new people. Your child may be going to a new school with their existing friends – but that can bring problems too. Their old friends may want to meet new people and your child may be left behind feeling betrayed. Transition is not just about friendships, though. Your child may worry about homework, getting lost, bullying, the pressure on them, being organised, getting to school and teachers.

If you have worries about your child coping at secondary school do not let on to them that you do. However, do talk to them about the fears that they have and discuss with them what will be expected of them once they move to their new school. It can be a hard time for parents when their children start secondary school as they are forced to accept that their child is growing up and they will never again be their baby who depends solely on them.

Leading up to the transition

When children are in year six at primary school they generally have had one or two teachers that have taught them. They are familiar with their environment, the playground, the type and amount of homework set and will have hopefully built up a great group of friends that they can count on and trust. Then, in spring they find out which school they are going to go to and seek out who will be going to the same school as them. Suddenly new alliances are made because the children who are all going to the same school want to get to know each other better and provide each other with a sense of security and comfort of not being on their own. Knowing which school your child is going to may make them feel insecure as they realise that in a few months they will be leaving the comfort zone of their friends, teachers, etc.

Moving schools is a big transition and it happens just as children are approaching puberty so they have to cope with an enormous amount of emotions as well as having surging hormones – not an easy task. It can be difficult to tell if the stress that they are feeling is related to the transition or whether it is their hormones. I would say it is likely to be transition stress if your child is like this during the months preceding them starting secondary school. We need to give them love and support at this time as well as giving them some space to deal with both changes.

Making new friends

Does your child find it difficult to make new friends or do they think they do? It may have been some time since they last made a new friend. Get them to think back.

Was it on their first day at school? I doubt it. It was more likely to be when they joined a new club or when they were out in the park and ended up chatting to a child who they did not know before but now they live out of each other's pockets.

Remind them of this time when they say they are worried about making new friends. Can they remember how they struck up a conversation? What questions did they ask, how did they respond to the other child? The type of questions they could ask new friends might include, 'Which school did you go to?', 'Could you show me how to …', 'Who do you know?' or 'Do you know what we have to do?'

What kind of manner did your child present themselves in? Were they polite or rude? What did their face look like – for example, were they smiling? Non-verbal communi-cation and body language is very important when making new friends. Crossing your arms gives out the message you are not interested in the person. As for smiling – well, there is nothing wrong in looking approachable. Reminiscing with your child about when they last made a new friend will make them feel good and ready to go out and do it again.

They may seem to think that they are the only one who is going to their new secondary school who does not know anyone else. Explain to them that most children who are moving to secondary school are going to have to make new friends, even if one or two of them already know each other. Even children who know others going to the same school as them may not know these 'acquaintances' very well and may be looking forward to meeting a new group of friends.

What does your child fear the most when making new friends? Is it that they are not going to be accepted for who they are?

Remind them that they cannot pretend to be something they are not. Imitation does not work. Other children will like them for who they are and it may take some time for them to meet those like-minded, accepting people. I would advise them to be friendly with lots of people and not to rush into having a best friend or a group initially. The first group or person they meet may not be the right person or group for your child.

If they do not think that they have anything to offer potential friends, remind them that they are great friend material and that it will not take long for them to make some. Get them to think about themselves and their likes and their dislikes, what they are good at and what they are not so good at. If your child knows who they are they can confidently say, 'I really like football but I am not so keen on playing tag'. They are then letting the other person they are talking to know a little bit about them and lots of these little 'bits' build up a picture of who they are and trust and friendship can begin.

It can also be a good idea for you to get them to talk to you about their attributes so they can remind themselves of the type of person they are. For example, 'I am helpful, outgoing, honest, trustworthy, fun, etc.' These qualities are things that other people look for in a friend. It may be a good idea for them to write these attributes on a piece of paper and for them to put it on their bedroom cupboard door to have a daily affirmation of how great they are and that they can be a good friend. If you look back at Chapter 6 on self-esteem there are lots of other exercises outlined which you can do with your child to remind themselves of who they are.

A healthy self-esteem is important to make friends. If your child had a bad time at primary school you will need to build up their self-esteem before secondary school starts so they feel strong and able to make friends and deal with new situations. Support them through the ups and downs of forming new friendships and reassure them that they will soon make new friends whom they will cherish as much as their old ones.

Old friendships

Children worry about the friendships that they forged in primary school. They hope that they will stay in touch, but they also worry about whether they will have enough time to still fit them into their lives. What with new friends to make and possibly a much longer day with more homework, will it be possible? We have to be honest with them and tell them that it may be hard for them to stay in touch with their old friends, but it is possible to keep those special people in their life. If both parties make an effort then the friendships can be kept alive. You can help them by making sure your child has time to see their old friends at the weekends or during the holidays. You could even set up a Skype or MSN account so they can keep in touch. Explain to them that if the friendship is strong enough it will survive through secondary school and beyond.

Homework

There are three main things that your child could be concerned about. The first is the amount of homework that they are now going to receive, the second is whether they are going to be able to do it and the third is how they are going to fit it into their week.

Regarding the amount of homework, explain to them that there may be more homework but hopefully the amount the teachers set will not be unreasonable. Ask them what they can do if they feel they have too much.

> *Andy, once he had settled into secondary school, found that he felt overwhelmed by the amount of homework so we chatted through some ideas of what he could do. After looking through the ideas he said, 'Well I can either do nothing and feel like it is all too much or I can speak to the teacher and ask for an extension or maybe see if my teacher has any other ideas.' He spoke to his teacher and he was not unreasonable. He re-visited the amount he was giving out for the whole class, which took the pressure off them all.*

What can you do to help your child when they say that they cannot do the work, if they say they don't understand it and they are afraid of telling the teacher that they feel this way? Can they think of another way of getting the work done without asking the teacher for help? One option is for them to ask one of their friends who they trust and see if they can help. Maybe they know what they are doing and they could explain it to them. Another option is for you to sit with them and guide them through what they have to do.

However, in either case it does not inform the teacher that your child does not understand the work that has been set. Encourage your child to tell the teacher and explain to them that not everyone understands everything the first time. Relate this to something they have learnt how to do – like riding a bike or crossing the road. They had to be shown several times before they got it right.

The work will be harder and will challenge your child and they need to realise that. It is also important to explain to them that not all the work will be exciting or interesting but it still has to be done.

The third thing your child may worry about is how they are going to fit all the homework into their schedule, given that they receive homework most nights for different subjects, all with different hand-in dates. Some of it will be project work that may take place over several weeks, while other pieces may have to be in the following day. I have to say that I see a lot of children starting secondary school struggling with the different deadlines. If your child is, ask them what they think of using a homework diary or having a homework plan near their work area. A homework diary can document what homework they have received, the details of the homework and how much time they need to spend on each subject. Every night they can see what has to be in the following day and make sure they have done that homework.

A homework plan is a little bit different. It is a plan that is kept at home and can be stuck on their bedroom wall or cupboard. It can be very simple and look like this:

HOMEWORK PLAN

	MON	TUES	WED	THURS	FRI	SAT	SUN
Day to do	English Maths	French			History		Art
Day to hand in	History	English Maths	French	Art			

Your child will then know what homework they have to do on which day and when it has to be handed in

Being organised

Primary school is quite easy when it to comes to organisation but secondary school is a different story, mainly because we want our children to be more responsible for their belongings and timings. The school will also expect students to manage them. We therefore need to encourage our children to organise themselves rather than for us to organise them. Your child may voice their concerns about not being ready in time for the bus and being late for school or you may notice they are finding it hard to get organised because they leave home forgetting or taking the wrong school books. If you notice that they are not as organised as they could be, ask them if they would like a bit of help; a little bit is all they need. They may need a new routine in the morning if their new school starts earlier or the journey is longer. How long do they think it will take for them to get ready in the morning? Get them to be realistic with the times they say. What are they doing in the morning that they could possibly do the night before? Perhaps they could pack their bag with the right school books and leave it by the front door at night.

Being organised does not come naturally and is a skill that has to be learnt. One way you can help them is by working out together what time they HAVE to get up by working backwards from the time they have to be at school.

For example: they have to be at school at 8.30 am

1 10 minutes to shower
2 5 minutes to dress
3 20 minutes for breakfast
4 10 minute walk to bus stop
5 15 minute bus ride

They then know that they need an hour to get ready from getting up to starting their school day.

I saw a boy called Daniel several years ago. He needed a system so he could remember what to take to school. I asked him when he got his bag ready and he said at night. What did he need to put in his bag? He understood that he needed the right books and homework to hand in. What were the consequences if he forgot his books or homework? He said he would get told off for handing the homework in late and possibly get a detention for forgetting his books. Did he want this to happen? No. How could he stop this from happening? He could remember his books and home-work. How could he do this? He could say to himself, 'I do not want to get into trouble. I need to remember my books and homework.' He could also put a big note on the inside of his bedroom door that said: 'BOOKS, HOMEWORK!' as another reminder.

Another issue Daniel had was with changing his books between lessons. Every break time he would go to his locker and put in the books which he no longer needed but forget to take out those for the next lesson. To help remind him to change books, he made a big yellow sign saying, 'BOOKS' on the inside of his locker alongside his school timetable. Both reminders really helped and it saved him getting into trouble so often.

How can you help your child to be organised for school and happy with their schedule?

Getting to school

If your child worries about getting to school find out exactly what it is that troubles them. Is it the long journey, not remembering the number of the bus or perhaps even walking into school on their own? What would they like to do to alleviate some of this anxiety? Suggest that perhaps they could go with friends to get the bus or walk together so that it is not so daunting going into school alone.

It may be the first time your child has travelled to school by bus or train. Make sure they know exactly where to board the bus or train and where to get off. Perhaps you could do a dummy run with them?

Teachers

Your child will be going from being taught by very few teachers to having a different one for each subject. That can be daunting for them as each teacher may have a different teaching style and some may be stricter than others. If your child is worried about their new teachers it is probably because they don't think they will get on with all of them or that the teachers won't like them. Explain to your child that there is no getting away from having more teachers and that they will have to learn to tolerate and respect each one, even if they do not like them all.

Bullying

If your child was bullied at their previous school reassure them that it does not mean they will be bullied at secondary school. I would not go into too much detail about bullying with them but let them see that moving to secondary school is a new start. Remind them of all the good things about school and the new opportunities that lie ahead for them. Those opportunities may be to learn a new language or musical instrument, go on field trips, etc.

Getting lost

Secondary school may be a lot bigger than your child's primary school and there is always a chance they will get lost. In fact, I can almost guarantee it. If your child is worried about this, reassure them that there will be lots of other children who get lost around the school and that the teachers are fully aware that this may happen and they may be late for lessons. It is okay to get lost and, if they do, what could they do? Perhaps they could ask an older student or a teacher for directions or to prevent them getting lost perhaps they could have a map of the school.

Some children panic if they get lost. If your child does, teach them breathing techniques and get them to think of the all the options of what they could do in the situation.

Putting pressure on themselves

Your child may have been with the same children from reception to year six and consider the children they grew up with to be their friends. There might have been a bit of competition among your child and their friends when it came to grades and ability and it may have been harmless fun. Now they are in secondary school there can be pressure put upon them by their new friends, teachers, possibly by you or even by themselves. If they feel the pressure you will know about it as it is likely to be showing in their emotions.

Possibly they are being bad-tempered or spending longer over their work. Ask them how they are coping with their new life and routine. If they feel like they are drowning and cannot cope with the school work, after school activities and social life – or lack of it – talk to them about what can give. Which activities are most important to them? Would they like to have more time seeing friends? Secondary school is harder and therefore it is important to get the balance right so that children are not stretching themselves beyond what is practical.

Settling into secondary school life is not easy for all children. If your child finds it tough remind them that it takes time to adjust to a new situation. They will make mistakes and get things wrong but they also will get lots of things right and each mistake is a learning experience.

Share your experience of starting secondary school with them and explain how you felt. What was different about your school and theirs?

> *How can you reduce the pressure in your child's life?*

Checklist

- There is a difference between being picked on and being bullied.
- Get children to think of the repercussions of not listening in class.
- Your child knows when is best for doing their homework.
- Being organised takes planning.
- Secondary school need not be daunting.

chapter ten

How to help your child with important life skills

> '*The cure for boredom is curiosity. There is no cure for curiosity*'
>
> DOROTHY PARKER

This chapter is a miscellaneous one but it is just as important as the rest because it covers those life skills that, as parents, we want our children to have. A parent will approach me and say, 'My child does not have these life skills and I feel they need to have them. Please can you help me teach them to my child.' The skills are simply listed alphabetically, and not in any order of importance.

Admitting fault

'It wasn't me. It was their fault.' We hear these words too often. How can we teach our children to put their hands up and admit blame? What do they think is going to happen if they do? Generally nothing will happen as they will have shown us that they can take responsibility for their own actions. Of course there will always be circum-stances where an action warrants a punishment and that will all depend on the type of parenting you practise. We need to explain to our children that life is not about finding blame all the time; it is about finding out the truth, and the truth always gets us in less trouble than lies. Ask your child what they are scared of by making an admission. Get them to practise owning up – perhaps give them a time limit to own up to what they did and that if they do so in the time then no one will be in trouble or the punishment may be reduced. For example, if they have been throwing rubbish on the floor. When you question your child if it is their rubbish and they say no and you may see from the look in their eyes that it was them, give them five minutes to own up. It is much easier to blame someone else than to 'take the rap' but is it the right thing to do?

> *Jessica used to always stomp off when something was her fault. It was her way of coping with the embarrassment of doing something wrong. We looked together at other things she could do instead of running away:*
>
> * *She could apologise and continue what she was doing.*
> * *She could apologise and leave the situation.*
>
> *Jessica decided she could apologise, mean it and continue with whatever she was doing. I cannot say that she found*

> *this the easiest thing to do in the world but she tried really*
> *hard to do it and continues to do so.*

It is also very interesting when children apologise when you know it is not their fault. If your child does this then it can be a sign of low self-esteem. You can help raise their self-esteem by working through some of the exercises from Chapter 6. With a healthy self-esteem, your child will realise that they should only apologise when they have personally done something wrong rather than taking the blame because they think it is always their fault.

Boredom

Some children find it hard to amuse themselves. They may be used to being entertained, being busy all the time or Mum, Dad and siblings being around to play. It is good for children to be bored as boredom can encourage creativity and imagination. If you have a child who complains they are bored, ask them what they would like to do. How could they help themselves to be less bored? What do they like doing? Can they do it on their own? The ideal answer would be yes.

Boredom can infringe on what other people are doing. If you have a bored child who goes in pursuit of a sibling to play with them when the sibling wants to get on with other things then your 'bored' child may get annoyed with them and an argument may start. The other downside to boredom is moaning and that can get us down, too!

Harry used to pick on his sister when he was bored. He would end up hurting her and then get into trouble. Did he like getting into trouble? No. So how could he avoid this happening? What could he do to keep himself busy and out of mischief? We made a list:

- *Read.*
- *Do some arts and crafts.*
- *Ask his sister if she wanted to play something.*
- *Play with his Lego.*
- *Play his favourite game on the PlayStation.*
- *Draw.*

Were all those things on his list possible for him to do without parental consent or involvement? Yes. He wrote out his list and I asked him where he could put it to remind himself of all the things he could do when he is bored. He said the wall in his bedroom was the best place for it and when he was bored he could go into his bedroom and see what he could do. Having something to do meant he would be less inclined to annoy his sister.

Ethan also used to get bored and could never think of anything to play. His mum was sick of him walking around unable to amuse himself. He made a list of things he liked doing, but instead of using the list to remind him to find something to do at that time, he would take out a game, book or activity at night so that in the morning, the time he felt most bored, he had something in his bedroom that could amuse him straightaway.

In the case of both Harry and Ethan, preparation was key to stop the boredom and having the lists reminded them that there was something they could be getting on with. For Harry, having the list in a prominent place worked.

I think if children have an issue finding something to occupy them first thing in the morning then it is a good idea to leave something out – books, crafts or leave the computer on if you have the appropriate internet security settings. It means they do not have to disturb you at an unreasonable hour.

Decision making

Some children find it a real chore to make a decision. They find it difficult because they think there is always a wrong and a right answer to a question. Some children like making decisions because they are not bothered by the outcome of them as they are easy-going, and some children want to please others and so let them make decisions for them rather than possibly go against another child's needs. There are also children who think that they should be making all the decisions that involve them and children who are desperate to make more but are not allowed to by their parents or peers.

If your child thinks there is a right and wrong answer to a decision

You can explain to them that there is not a right or wrong answer. Whatever decision your child makes it will always be one that they can learn from. It can be a simple decision like choosing an ice-cream flavour – vanilla or chocolate. They are the ones who are going to eat it so which is more appealing to them?

THE TOOL TO USE

Decision-making tool

1 If you know your child finds decision making hard give them a choice of a couple of options, 'Do you want me to buy these trousers or this skirt for you?'

2 Make it clear to them when they make their choice that they have to stick to it as it makes it harder for everyone around them if they change their mind later.

3 If your child finds that they have made the wrong decision for them on this occasion they will have learnt from the experience.

Children who aren't bothered about making a decision

Decisions are not going to be made for them all their life. Even if they are not bothered about what they do, everyone has an opinion about something and they should voice that.

Natalie was a client of mine who would go along with the actions of her friends and family. She did not seem to care about what she did. Her parents wanted her to speak up as they were getting a little frustrated by her 'non-views' and wanted to know what made her happy, what made her excited. I asked her to write a list of what made her happy and what she liked doing. Her list was considerably longer than expected and it looked like this:

- *Cinema.*
- *Eating sushi.*
- *Spending time with Mum.*
- *Seeing my best friend.*
- *Bowling.*
- *Making cakes.*
- *Playing DS.*
- *Making jewellery.*

I wanted to know why, when her mum said, 'What type of food shall we eat tonight when we go out for dinner?' and she said, 'I don't mind', why she did not say, 'I fancy sushi.'

Or if her friends asked her what she fancied doing that day, why didn't she say, 'Bowling or the cinema?' I explained the importance of making decisions and that if everything was always decided for her then eventually she would be unhappy as she would never get to have or do what she wanted. Did she want to get what she wanted? Yes. Did she want to try out making decisions and see what happened when she did? Yes. I suggested she thought to herself when she was asked a question, 'If I don't decide I will have to do what the others want and I won't get to do/eat what I want. I should choose.'

The next time I saw her she said she had found it difficult at first but the day before she had come back to see me she'd told her mum she wanted to see her best friend when asked what she fancied doing.

If your child does not want to make decisions for fear of upsetting others

There will always be people pleasers and one way children can please others is by letting them get their own way. It is good for them to be considerate of other people's thoughts and feelings, but it is just as important for children to make sure that they get what they want or need, too. It can be deeply frustrating for them if they are always putting their needs last. One way in which you can help your child toughen up and voice their opinion is to let them see how you do it. Model your own decision-making skills when your children are around so they can watch and learn from you. For example, if one of your friends asks you to pick up their child from school and take them home but you are in a rush to get your child to an after school activity and it will make you really late say, 'No'. Tell your child what happened and explain to them that we cannot always compromise our needs.

If your child wants to make all of the decisions

We want to instil a sense of responsibility into our children and empower them to make their own decisions but what can we do when they think that they should be making all of them? Well, we can sit down and talk to them about the role parents have when it comes to making decisions and that there are different levels of decision making. Explain to your child that you will allow them to make choices that you think are relevant for their age and lifestyle. Most of these will be your choices. The big decisions, like what time they go to bed, how we spend our family money, where we go on holiday are ours to make as parents; how to spend their birthday money, what they make out of Lego and what cereal to eat for breakfast are theirs.

If your child is desperate to make more decisions but is not allowed

Children will complain to me that they are not allowed to make many decisions and they feel like their parents do not trust them. It may be that their parents are controlling or that they are scared of the decisions their child may make. You can help them by letting go a bit and giving them the freedom to make some of their own decisions, even if they are bad ones. Yes, they might get emotionally or physically upset or hurt but they will learn from their own mistakes and that will teach them more than years of lecturing from you.

> A rather simple example of this is Leah, who wanted to be able to choose what clothes she was going to wear at the weekends. Her mum insisted that she choose them for her because she felt that the clothes Leah wanted to wear were inappropriate for the weather or for what they were going to do the following day. This made Leah upset because she wanted to do it. I spoke with Leah and asked her what she could do. She said she could ask her mum what their plans were for the next day, choose her own clothes and if they were wrong for the day she would take responsibility for being too hot, too cold, too wet. Her mum agreed and it meant that Leah was able to make a decision. Making the right or wrong decisions empowered Leah, which is what she needed to feel.

As you make decisions talk with your children about them. Explain your thought process of how you came to make a decision and discuss your priorities and motives. Tell them about decisions you've made in the past – the good, bad and hard ones. The beauty of sharing our stories is that our children can learn the easy way what we learnt the hard way. Take the time to walk your children through the process of making a decision and remember, they will learn more from a little trial and error than they will if you make every decision for them. Having strong problem-solving and decision-making skills will help your children learn what they need to be strong decision makers in their adult life.

Finally, if our children do not make decisions they will not get what they want and may be unhappy with the outcome. A great part of decision making for them is knowing what they want and that can be the tricky part. Many children do not know what they want, especially when faced with lots of good choices. We can help them by giving them choices of two. For example, 'We can go the park or we can go swimming'. The decision-making process for them can be made easier this way.

Embracing change

Some children find it incredibly difficult to embrace change and find it hard to adapt and adjust to new situations. If your child is like this you can help them to see that not all change is bad and scary and sometimes they have to accept that and they cannot do anything about it. For example, they cannot do anything about their parents splitting up or moving from primary to secondary school. If you find your child is going to be affected by change then you can prepare them by talking about it, answering their questions and discussing their worries. Children generally like to know what is coming next so that they can start working out in their minds what is going to happen and when. They can mentally prepare themselves for the change.

Manners

Most parents want their children to have good manners. When I say manners, I mean 'please' and 'thank you' and generally being considerate of other people. When a child bumps into another person we would like them to say, 'Sorry', regardless of the bump being accidental or intentional.

Manners are important for a few reasons. Good manners can say a lot about your child and their upbringing. If you can teach your child good manners it can make them more respectful towards others and they are more likely to be treated with respect themselves. There is nothing nicer than hearing a 'please' or a 'thank you' from a child. Politeness can make a great first impression.

But what do you do when you have a child who forgets their manners on a regular basis. How do you re-educate them? You can do several things:

- You can make sure you always use your manners, setting them a good example.
- If they forget you could prompt them by saying, 'Did you forget something?' or you could just pretend you did not hear what they were saying because they missed out their 'please'.
- Make it clear to your child what is expected of them in the manners department.
- Ask them how they are treated by their friends and how they should treat their friends. If they say their friends are polite to them, ask them what that means to them. Is being polite something they think they do enough of?
- Ask them how they would like to be remembered after they have met someone for the first time?
- Talk to them about the importance of politeness when it comes to play dates or when they are invited to a friend's house for the first time. If they want to be invited back they will have to remember these types of things.

Which manners do you feel are the most important for your child to have?

Table manners

I also want to mention table manners here because I think it fits in well with the niceties we want our children to display. Table manners are important because we want to be able to take our children out to eat and not be embarrassed when they eat at friends' houses. I know mothers cringe when they see their children abandoning their knife and fork and replacing them with their fingers. If a child does not understand which manners are required at the table I would ask them why they think they have cutlery and question them about how they think they should act at the table. If you want your child to eat nicely then one idea is to put some rules in place. For about three or four years now we have had rules in our household for mealtimes. The number of rules drawn up at the beginning was very long since the whole family added their thoughts. There were over 20 rules and we managed to get them down to 5:

1. No talking when you are eating (i.e. with your mouth full).
2. Sit nicely on your chair.
3. You have to ask to leave the table.
4. You have to wait for everyone to eat their main course before getting dessert.
5. Use your cutlery.

These rules were written up on the kitchen noticeboard and I would ask my children what the rules were if I could see them starting to break them.

I am not saying that these specific rules should be used for everyone but if you sat down with your family and drew up five, what would they look like?

Negative thinking

We all think negatively sometimes about events happening in our lives or about ourselves. It is part of life. Some of us can cope with it and some of us can't. For children, though, it can be difficult for them to think positively when they have experienced someone putting them down or when they have not done so well at something. Negative thoughts creep into their minds easily and uninvited and they can be hard to get rid of.

When children believe that they are going to fail, they will unconsciously sabotage every opportunity to succeed. For instance, in a game of rounders they may not try or make an effort to win. They may play half-heartedly. After all, there is no chance that their team is going to win because they are part of 'that' team.

The same goes for when someone says something to your child that is deemed 'negative' and they take it to heart. For example, if someone calls them an idiot they may believe that they are. The word is internalised and they can think negatively about themselves. Negative thoughts can stop your child doing something that they want or have to do. They can see life as gloomy, not interesting and don't see anything good about themselves.

Jay was a negative thinker who went to an academic school. He was in year six and the school where he wanted to go next required him to sit an entrance exam. Jay sat the exam and did not get in. The school said that he could re-sit the exam as they believed he had the capability of passing. I saw him after he had sat the first exam and I could see he was upset. We talked about his feelings and why he thought he did not pass. He said he had not tried hard enough because he did not think he was capable of passing it. I asked him:

Did he want to get into the school? Yes.

Did he want to put the effort in and re-sit? Yes, but only if he passed.

What was making him think he would not pass? Because he failed this time and he could fail again.

How did he get into his existing school? He had sat an exam.

What does that tell him? He has done it before and he can do it again.

How could he think differently so that he put the effort in and could pass? He could think more positively and imagine himself at the new school, happy.

What would he think and say to himself to keep on going? He could think, 'I know I can do this; I am good enough and I will get in.'

Would that be enough to motivate himself to study hard and be confident that this time he really was going to do it? Yes.

We made a list of Jay's achievements and talked through the steps of what he needed to say to himself. I saw him for two sessions. The second time I saw him he shared with me his joy at passing the exam. It was a great feeling to hear that together we had lifted his confidence to do well and left his negative thoughts behind.

If your child finds themselves in the negative thinking trap what is it generally about?

Your child's negative thinking comes from their life experience but it can also come from you. Once they get into the cycle of having negative thoughts it can be difficult for them to snap out of them. How can you help them do this? Well, you can get them to look at what they are good at and what they are able to do. You can also try and get them to see that just because something bad has happened in the past, it does not mean that the experience is going to happen again. For example, if your child fell off a swing in the park and hurt themselves, they may think it will happen again so won't want to take the risk of going on another swing.

Negative thinking can stop children from doing new things. They can avoid difficult situations and even give up easily. 'I have tried but it did not work the first time therefore I cannot do it.' I have seen children who are really sad and it is because they have so many negative thoughts and beliefs. For example, they may say, 'I don't want to go to Ben's party because it will be rubbish' or 'I got a bad mark in the maths test and so I am not going to try any harder because I tried hard last time and I did not do well.'

If you have a negative thinker why not get them to list out what their negative thoughts are and look for the evidence for each one. Here is an example of what it might look like:

NEGATIVE THOUGHT	EVIDENCE THAT SUPPORTS IT	EVIDENCE THAT DOES NOT SUPPORT IT
I am rubbish at football	Missed goal	Scored in the game before, good tackler
I am never going to win the race	None	Won race last year
I know I am never going to do it	None	Not tried

This type of approach encourages balanced thinking. Balanced thinking is when you take a thought and turn it on its head. If someone calls your child stupid they can think to themselves, 'Okay so they called me stupid. Am I? No. Then I will not let it affect me.' Rather than them thinking that it was said it so it must be true. It is about being rational within or about a situation. Here are some other ideas of how you can help your negative thinker:

THE TOOL TO USE

Negative thoughts tool

1 Every time you catch your child verbalising a negative thought get them to reject it.

2 Get them to think of a positive one instead.

Like the stupid example I gave above, if they have been told they are 'stupid' maybe they could think to themselves, 'Actually, I am clever because I . . .'

- You could do an exercise with them where they make a list of negative thoughts about themselves or life and then get them to make a list of positive thoughts. This will help them see that life is not all doom and gloom. You can also do this visually by having a stick person with two speech bubbles coming out of their mouth – one bubble for the negative thoughts and one bubble for the positive thoughts.

- If you catch them saying that they are going to fail, get them to visualise that they will succeed instead. You can ask them what succeeding looks like. If they close their eyes can they imagine themselves jumping in the air and feeling really happy because they achieved something?

- Encourage them to write down their negative thoughts in a diary and then look for the evidence that dispels the negative thought. If they did this every night they would see how negative they were being and how positive they could be.

- Help them to say 'I can' instead of 'I can't'. Maybe consider 'can't' as a kind of swear word and they get a forfeit every time you catch them saying 'I can't'. Alternatively, they could be fined a penny that goes in a jar.

- Show them how to have a positive mental attitude by expressing delight at new experiences and embracing your own new challenges.

You may also have a child that magnifies the negative and says things like, 'Everyone hates me', when in fact there are a couple of people who dislike them. Talk to them about the reality so they can see that actually the statement they are making is not true.

Finally in this part about negative thinking I think it is important to mention attitude. There are children who don't seem to get enthusiastic about anything. If you have a child like this you can make them more positive by sitting down with them and looking at their whole life – school, friends, you, siblings, activities, etc. – and getting them to find something good about each part of their life. For example, you could ask them, 'What's good about having a sibling?', 'What's good about school?' and 'Which lesson or teacher?'

How is your child negative and which ideas could you put into action with them so they become full of positivity?

Responsibility and independence

Children can be cheeky things. They would have you running around after them 24 hours a day if you let them, but will they learn to stand on their own two feet this way? No. How can we make our children more responsible and able? Well, we can start by looking at what they are capable of. Think of your child's age and ability. What could they do for and by themselves?

- Make their bed?
- Make their lunch?
- Make plans with friends?
- Get dressed?
- Lay the table?

Melanie, aged eight, used to get annoyed with her mum because she would ask her to do jobs in the house which she did not want to do. She would spend time arguing with her mum when in fact she could have just got on with the job in hand and gone back to what she was doing before. I wanted to show her that what she was being asked to do was not unreasonable so I got her to make a list of what her mum had asked her to do and we listed the amount of time she thought it took. The list looked like this:

- *Empty dishwasher – 4 minutes.*

- *Lay table – 2 minutes.*
- *Make bed – 2 minutes.*
- *Tidy room – 10 minutes.*

I then asked her how long she argued over not wanting to do these chores for. She said 10 minutes each time. I asked her if it was and what could she have been doing in that time.' She got the message pretty quick. She could have had an extra 40 minutes to spend playing. Melanie took on board our conversation and when I saw her next she said she had started just doing what she was asked without a fuss and that it was good not to argue with her mum any more.

Another example of getting a child to be more independent is Ben. Ben, aged 11, did not feel happy because of his social life. His mum refused to make plans for him as she felt he was capable of doing this himself. I asked him what he thought he could do to improve it. What kind of social life did he want? How many plans a week? When – after school or at the weekend? How could he make plans? He said twice a week he would like to see his friends and that he could make plans when he saw them next. He was not bothered if it was after school or at the weekends. How did he want to spend his time with them? Playing X-box or going to the park. We tightened up his plan and decided that the next time he saw his friends he would suggest that they came to his house on a particular day to play on the

X-box. It took Ben a while to get going and make social plans given he was responsible for making them when he saw his friends. In order for his plan to really work, which he felt it wasn't, we went back over the options. He decided it would be a better idea if he called or texted his friends to make plans and then they would be less likely to forget about them. When I saw him next he said the texting was working much better and he was beginning to like making his own arrangements with friends.

Timekeeping

Lots of children find it hard to be organised. For whatever reason, they need help with timekeeping as being disorganised and not keeping to time will get them into trouble. If you have a child who is a bad timekeeper there are things you can do to help them, such as:

- Set an alarm for them to wake and get up (if they have to get to school). Maybe put the alarm clock as far away from the bed as possible so they have to actually get out of bed.
- Give them warnings as to how long they have before they have to be somewhere.
- Use sticky notes in their bedroom reminding them they have to do something by x time.
- Remind them yourself if they want you to.

- Ask them, 'Can you imagine what it says to the other person you are late for?' and 'How would you feel if someone was late meeting you?'

If your child is rushing you because they hate being late ask them what they think will be the consequences of being late.

Zak felt anxious when he was late for parties. He used to get tummy ache as he was worried that he would have to walk into the room alone and everyone would look at him. We talked about how he could change his thinking so that he was less worried about walking into a room full of friends. I suggested he thought, 'It does not matter if I am late. All my friends will be at the party and if everyone stares at me when I come in then I should think that is a good thing. They were waiting for me.' Zak tailored the thought into something that would work best for him and tried it out weeks later at a party. He felt that it had worked to some extent but that it would take some getting used to.

If timekeeping is important to you as a parent try and demonstrate good timekeeping. If you know that your child is very anxious about being late you can reduce their anxiety by trying to be on time wherever possible. For example, many children really worry when their parents are late to collect them from an activity.

Checklist

- Admitting blame shows maturity.
- Preparation relieves a child's boredom.
- It is better to make a wrong decision than none at all.
- Share your decision-making process with your child.
- Good manners can bring mutual respect.
- Challenge negative thoughts.
- Balance a negative thought with a positive one.
- Small domestic jobs can teach children responsibility and independence.

Conclusion

I hope you have enjoyed reading this book. Some of you may have read it from cover to cover and others of you may have dipped in and out of it when you have needed to. I hope you have managed to get some great ideas from it and feel able to try them out with your children with or without their knowledge. All the ideas I have mentioned in the book are ones that I use in my coaching sessions, but there are many more – if only I could list them all!

What I would like to say is that once you have decided on a course of action with your child stick with it and monitor how your child is getting on. I mentioned a notebook in the introduction. I think a notebook is a great way to track your child's progress, and yours too, so long as you date the developments. You are both taking on making real changes in your child's life, and your child may be more willing to make these changes if you show them that you are committed to helping them improve areas of their life with them. Don't give up; any change is difficult at the beginning but it will get easier. If there is no change after a month then it may be a good idea to look at another option to approach the issue your child is working on. Don't try and change everything at the same time. If your child has self-esteem issues and also has a problem with communication go with the one they want help with more urgently. Then when that issue looks like it is on the mend you can start talking about another one.

Be consistent, supportive, empowering, encouraging and give them confidence. Help them make positive changes in their lives.

Quick reference guide to all the tools

To help you find the tools easily, I have listed them below:

About the author

I have been a life coach for children since 2004. Prior to that, I worked in marketing for 10 years. I decided to change my work direction after I got married (and pregnant). Pregnancy gave me some time to reflect on who I was and what I wanted to do with the rest of my working life. I have always been able to stand on my own two feet, liked to solve any difficulties I had myself and took full responsibility for my actions. I realised that some of my friends didn't have the same sense of independence but didn't want to rely on other people to make decisions for them or to help them out of difficult situations. My friends would question me about how I managed to be so self-sufficient and would often ask me to help them out with their problems. I was very willing to help and got great satisfaction from being able to do this.

I realised that problem solving and creative thinking was something that I enjoyed doing and that with some formal training I could help other people with their problems and life issues. I had coached children informally at summer camps and youth organisations when I was in my teens and had really loved helping young people think for themselves. I decided post-children that I would change my career, as many mums do, and follow my passion. I re-trained as a life coach and set up my own business coaching children formally.

The coaching centre where I studied was surprised by my desire to work with children but did not discourage me from doing so, as they could see I had the right kind of personality to deal with children. Life coaching, as my tutors knew it, had only been successful with adults and they were unsure that coaching would work with children. I believed it could as children also have goals and ambitions. They also have problems that they find difficult to solve themselves. What they often don't have are the tools to achieve what they want on their own and that was where I would come in.

I am so pleased I followed my vision now because there is no better feeling than knowing I have changed a child's outlook on life or improved the way they look at things. I think it has also helped me in my role as a parent. I am more in tune with my children and spend a great deal of time with them talking about situations they find themselves in at school, with their friends, as well as their feelings.

To date, I have worked in a clinical setting, within schools and at home. My favourite and most successful place of work is in my own home. I have found that children respond better in the relaxed environment of my house. I think this is down to children seeing that I am part of a family – walls covered with photos, mismatched furniture and they see I am a 'normal' person.

I also write for many websites and teenage, women's and parenting magazines and contribute to local and national press and radio features. I have been involved in a teenage radio show where I was an 'agony aunt' and I am currently involved in a weekly parenting and family radio programme for Three Counties Radio. I run workshops for children at home and in schools and I am also a motivational speaker for young people. With a wide reach into the community, I feel I can make a huge difference to how children are living their lives and I can give parents an insight into what children really want from them – for me, that is what this book is all about!

Further information

If you have found this book resourceful but feel that your child could benefit from working with me then please do get in touch. If you visit my website, www.thekidscoach. org.uk, there is more information about me and my work. If you sign up for my monthly newsletter you will receive daily coaching ideas and tips to help your children understand who they are and help them grow into well-rounded adults.

You can also email me at Naomi@thekidscoach.org.uk, follow me on Twitter: http://twitter.com/thekidscoach and I also have a Facebook page where I post useful parenting-related blogs and articles – search for The Kids Coach on Facebook.

Good luck and remember, if you need me I am on the end of a phone.

Best wishes,
Naomi
The Kids' Coach

References

Page 13 *'We have two ears and one mouth so that we can listen twice as much as we speak'* Epictetus (c. AD 55–135)

A Greek philosopher who developed a system for teaching his students to practices stoicism in their daily lives. He taught how to strive for moral excellence to achieve eudaimonia.

Page 33 *'The secret to humour is surprise'* Aristotle (384–322 BC)

An ancient Greek philosopher, a student of Plato and teacher of Alexander the Great. He wrote on diverse subjects, including physics, poetry, biology and zoology, logic, rhetoric, politics and government and ethics.

Page 34 *'According to research, 93% of effective communication is non-verbal, 55% is expressed by body language and 38% by tone, which leaves only 7% for the spoken word'* Professor Albert Mehrabian

Professor Albert Mehrabian has pioneered the understanding of communications since the 1960s. He received his PhD from Clark University and in 1964 commenced an extended career of teaching and research at the University of California, Los Angeles. He currently devotes his time to research, writing and consulting as Professor Emeritus of Psychology, UCLA. Mehrabian's work featured strongly in the mid to late 1900s in establishing early understanding of body language and non-verbal communications.

Page 36 *'Without self-confidence we are as babes in the cradle'* Virginia Woolf (1882–1941), *A Room of One's Own*

English author, essayist and publisher regarded as one of the most influential modernist writers of the 20th century.

Page 73 *'When dealing with people, remember you are not dealing with creatures of logic, but with creatures of emotion, creatures bristling with prejudice, and motivated by pride and vanity'* Dale Carnegie (1888–1955)

A popular and enduring author on poise and concentration. His most popular book was *How to Win Friends and Influence People*, which was first published in 1936.

Page 102 *'True happiness consists not in the multitude of friends, but in their worth and choice'* Samuel Johnson (1709–1784), *Johnson's Lives of the Poets*, vol. i–iv

Essayist, lexicographer, biographer and poet.

Page 135 *'Never bend your head. Hold it high. Look the world straight in the eye'* Helen Keller (1880–1968)

An American author, political activist and lecturer who proved how language could liberate the blind and the deaf.

Page 148 *'Always be a first-rate version of yourself, instead of a second-rate version of somebody else'* Judy Garland (1922–1969)

American actress and singer.

Page 157 *'If we have no peace, it is because we have forgotten that we belong to each other'* Mother Teresa August (1910–1997)

Author, religious leader, Nobel peace prize winner, Christian saint and missionary.

Page 181 *'Whatever brawls disturb the street, there should be peace at home'* Isaac Watts (1674–1748)

An English pastor, preacher, poet and non-conformist hymn writer. He wrote over 700 hymns praising the Creator, His works and Word.

Page 241 *'The cure for boredom is curiosity. There is no cure for curiosity'* Dorothy Parker (1893–1967)

American author, humourist, poet and wit.

Acknowledgements

As this book is about communication I think it is only right that I thank the people who have made it possible. My first acknowledgement is a heartfelt thank you to all the children who have given me the opportunity to work with them. You made me realise this book had to be written and it would not have been possible without you. My next thank you goes to Nick Coffer, my conduit. I cheekily asked if you thought your literary agent would mind if I contacted her to see what she thought about my idea, and lo and behold she took me on. Thank you, Clare, for believing that this book had a place on a bookshelf. It has been really great to work with you and I hope we get to do it again soon! It has also been great to work with you, Susanna. You have been a wonderful editor, have had faith in my writing ability and I feel so privileged to have worked with you and all the team at Vermilion. You have made the publishing process easy and trouble-free. It has been an adventure and one I have enjoyed.

I want to thank Richard Maun, my avid writer friend. Richard, thank you for your help and guidance with pre-publishing protocol. As you know, your advice was invaluable. I also want to thank Helen for quote checking, providing the admin support I have needed over the past six months and doing such a great job helping me promote the book together with the publicity team at Vermilion. You have been fab.

My friends, the proofreaders, Mel, Rachel and Becky – thank you for spending your free time reading the manuscript. Along with Dana, Lorraine, Miriam and Lana you have been amazing sounding boards for my ideas and nourishing my thoughts. I would also like to thank all my other lovely girlfriends and the mums at school (you know who you are) who have helped me with childcare and listened to me talk endlessly and passionately about the book. It is so good of you to constantly ask me how things are going, too. You have all kept me going.

Mum and Dad, thank you for taking my endless calls at all hours and I apologise for going for days without returning yours. Life has been wonderfully crazy at times. Along with my sisters, Mandy, Penny and Jodie, thank you for sharing the ride and for being incredibly supportive.

Finally, I want to thank my husband, who has cheered me on from the sidelines and believed in me to do something that I am so passionate about. I also want to thank my well-coached boys, E and K. Boys, I know you don't really understand what I do when I say I help children and make them happier, but one day I hope you will. I am very proud of you both and I hope you will be proud of me and my work. I hope you both continue to grow as thoughtful, kind, generous, confident, considerate, spirited individuals.